Guerrilla Learning

Guerrilla Learning

How to Give Your Kids a Real Education
With or Without School

GRACE LLEWELLYN

AMY SILVER

John Wiley & Sons, Inc.
New York • Chichester • Weinheim • Brisbane • Singapore • Toronto

Published by John Wiley & Sons, Inc.
Published simultaneously in Canada

This publication is designed to provide accurate and authoritative information in regard to the subject matter covered. It is sold with the understanding that the publisher is not engaged in rendering professional services. If professional advice or other expert assistance is required, the services of a competent professional person should be sought.

Library of Congress Cataloging-in-Publication Data

Llewellyn, Grace.
   Guerrilla learning : how to give your kids a real education with or without school/ Grace Llewellyn and Amy Silver.
      p. cm.
   Includes bibliographical references and index.
   ISBN 0-471-34960-7 (pbk. : alk. paper)
      1. Education—Parent participation—United States. 2. Alternative education—United States. 3. Home schooling—United States. I. Silver, Amy. II. Title.

LB1048.5 .L54 2001
371.04—dc21   2001017917

Printed in the United States of America

10 9 8 7 6 5 4 3 2 1

To
CARSIE AND ELIJAH

Contents

Acknowledgments

AUTHORS' NOTE:

Just before *Guerrilla Learning* went to press, we were dismayed to learn that John Taylor Gatto was writing a book with a very similar title. We borrowed the "guerrilla" metaphor from Mr. Gatto in the first place, and the last thing we want to do is take credit for his ideas or his language. On the contrary, we admire his work; we urge anyone who is interested in the ideas expressed in this book to seek out and read Mr. Gatto's books as well. Further details are available at www.john taylorgatto.com.

AMY:

I thank my parents, Leslie Silverman and Gloria Asher, who raised me in a home filled with books, music, conversation, and scientific gadgets. My former husband, Brad Blanton, showed me how to give children true freedom and unconditional love. I am very grateful to Beth and Ray Kljajic, my sister and brother-in-law, for their generous support while Grace and I wrote this book.

My coauthor, Grace Llewellyn, profoundly influenced my views on education when I stumbled across her books in the early 1990s. I thank her also for agreeing to write with me and for bringing the possibility of a life of joy and freedom to so many teenagers (including my daughter, Carsie). My friend Hugo Elfinstone helped me to find a truer writing voice. Susan Gushue read a draft of the manuscript and blessed me with her feedback and insight; it was during our conversations over the last fifteen years that many of the ideas presented here were refined. I am grateful to her family and the other families who allowed us to share their stories. I also thank my dad, Leslie

Silverman, for his careful reading of the manuscript and his thought-ful feedback.

I appreciate the members of the Alternative Education Resource Organization and Richard Prystowsky of *Paths of Learning* magazine, who provided us with much direct and indirect assistance both in helping us locate families to interview and in teaching us about alter-native education generally.

My friends Grace Tiffany, Michele Sterline, Maryann Altman, Chris Eichmann, Tina Oehser, Bart Parrott, Sandy Wood, Shari Rowles, and Marjie Gibson helped me keep my sanity, my health, and my car pool together during the writing. My deepest appreciation goes to Jane Mullen and the staff and families of Hearthstone School in Sperryville, Virginia, for living their dream of "education with a heart." I thank my children and stepkids—Shanti, Amos, Carsie, and Elijah—for educating me daily about the beauty of the human spirit.

Finally, I thank our agents, Jane Dystel and Charles Myer, for their support and guidance, and the estimable Elizabeth Zack at Wiley, who had reminded me what a true editor is.

GRACE:

Not yet a mother myself, I couldn't have written about parenting on my own. Yet collaboration scares me. I'm neurotically independent. So I feel tremendously fortunate that Amy invited me to work with her. When she phoned me, we'd never met, though we had corresponded. Something about the way she spoke that day—her openness, her wit, and her obvious wisdom—inspired me to say "yes" to her proposal within a matter of hours. And I've never regretted that "yes." Amy's enthusiasm and initiative; her accepting and vulnerable way of befriending me; her many great ideas and insights; her skills as a writer; and the inspiring job she does of being the quintessential Guerrilla Learning mom—all these made the whole project a plea-sure, although it came during a somewhat traumatic, transitional period in my personal life. She deserves much more credit for this book than I do. That's not self-deprecation, just fact. She did more work and kept us on track, though her life, too, was in great upheaval while we wrote.

I am unspeakably grateful to Taber Shadburne, my closest friend and my mentor. He *always* dropped whatever he was doing and said "yes" when I asked him to listen to a draft; his background as a psychotherapist and his deeply empathetic way of relating to children heavily influenced this book.

While writing, I thought with much gratitude of my own parents, David and Gai Llewellyn. When I was a child, they abundantly and generously honored what Amy and I came to identify as the "Five Keys of Guerrilla Learning": opportunity, timing, freedom, interest, and support.

It's a pleasure to thank our insightful editor, Elizabeth Zack, for her careful reading and her astute suggestions.

I appreciate the many families and teenagers who sent personal stories that illustrated our points. Although in the end we weren't able to use all of this material (partly because we shifted directions several times midcourse), each of these people increased my understanding of Guerrilla Learning and so helped shape this book.

Finally, sincere thanks to two geniuses for their dedicated, skillful help with my other projects while I was busy with this one: Skip Bergin and Lesly Cormier.

Guerrilla Learning

Introduction

It is in fact nothing short of a miracle that the modern methods of
instruction have not yet entirely strangled the holy curiosity of inquiry.
—*Albert Einstein*

Your children don't seem as bright-eyed or vital as they did a few
years ago. You remember their excitement about learning to
walk, learning to talk, playing with sand and water, seeing snow
for the first time. Somehow, you think you expected more for
them. You know there's nothing really wrong with your kids—
their friends are no different.

Your son is withdrawn and you know he doesn't participate much
in class. You worry that he's losing out and wonder what you can
do to help him reclaim his self-esteem and continue his academic learning despite his disengaging from school.

You don't think there's anything especially wrong with your kids'
teachers or their school—but you want *more* for them. More
learning, more growth, more inspiration, more opportunity. . . .

Your kids spend hours and hours each night doing homework.
Their school no longer has recess. They, the other students at
their school, and even the teachers are anxious and overwhelmed by new tests that have been introduced in your state.
You wonder what's really going on: Were the schools doing that
poorly? Who decided what's on the tests? Why is this happening
when the teachers don't even seem to want it?

1

When you say "What did you do in school today?" your kids say "Nothing." When you ask "How was school?" they say "Fine," or "Boring," or "Stupid." You think, "Well, that's just the way of the world. That's what I said when my parents asked me. And come to think of it, it did usually feel pretty inconsequential, pretty nondescript. . . . I wonder, couldn't school be more inspiring?"

Last year your daughter had a great teacher—she loved school and was eager to jump out of bed almost every morning. This year it's another story. What can you do to help her have another great year—even without a great teacher?

Your seven-year-old son isn't reading yet. His teacher seems concerned and wants him to go to summer school. In fact, she has suggested he may have a learning disability. You're worried about him falling behind, but you're also upset about the pressure he seems to be feeling. What are your options?

Another student is bullying your son—or an immature teacher has made him a scapegoat. Consequently, your son is afraid of the whole school experience. You've basically given up hope that he'll learn much this year. What can you do to help him stay "afloat" academically until he regains his confidence?

You worry about your kids' futures when you hear pessimistic predictions about the economy or when you read about how competitive colleges are these days.

Whether your kids get good grades or bad grades, they seem to turn off their brains as soon as they get home from school. You know that's "normal," but it bothers you.

Your kids seem fearful: about school, or reading, or working with numbers, or speaking in front of people.

Your son has been diagnosed as having attention deficit disorder.

Your daughter has been diagnosed as having a learning disorder.

Your kids are creative, but school isn't doing much to help them develop their creativity.

Your kids *used* to be creative, but it's been years since they wrote a poem or painted a picture.

Your kids don't actually seem very creative. You'd like to encourage them to develop artistically.

Your kids are stressed out. Their faces look tight and pinched, or they fight more than you imagine is healthy, or they don't sleep well, or they sleep too much. . . .

Your kid is having a hard time focusing at school because of

- feeling distracted by social cliques and pressure
- a peer culture that mocks kids who take learning seriously
- fear of violence
- a personality clash or conflict with a teacher

Your kids work hard, and you think they're bright, but they don't get good grades. You're worried that their self-esteem will suffer as a result, that eventually they may give up.

Your kids don't work hard, but they get good grades. You're worried that they're not being stretched or challenged.

Your kids don't work hard, and they get bad grades. You're worried about failure, about consequences later in their lives, and about their self-esteem.

Your kids work hard and get good grades, and you're worried that they're overachievers—that they're setting themselves up for a lifetime of workaholism, of stress, of moving too fast.

Your kids are having trouble with some basic skill—reading, writing, math computation. They and you are worried about them getting hopelessly behind.

You'd probably never try homeschooling, but you see yourself as deeply involved in your kids' education, and you are always interested in ideas about learning.

In short: You want to help your kids get a good education—and you fear that, for whatever reason, right now they're not getting a good enough one.

Have we read your mind? Once? More than once?

No? Pass this book along to your favorite cousin, or stick it back on the shelf already so someone else can buy it.

Yes? Maybe this book is for you. But not unless you also can answer "yes" to two more important questions:

1. Are you willing to hold an open mind while we unravel and analyze a system you were raised basically to trust: the American school system? And not just the system itself, but the thinking that goes along with it, to which you may feel attached? Such as: Grades are important. Your kids should work hard and do well in school. If they don't, they'll have a hard time succeeding in life.

2. Furthermore: Supposing that what we say makes sense to you, *are you willing to change*? To make fundamental shifts in the way *you* live and learn, and also in the way you relate to your kids about their learning?

No? Please refer to the earlier line regarding favorite cousins and returning books to shelves for other customers.

Yes? Welcome to *Guerrilla Learning*! We wrote this book for you.

Now, before you count your chickens and break out the champagne:

We *don't* promise to:

- Help you get your kids to get better grades
- Get your kids into Harvard
- Tell you how to get your kids to do their homework
- Get your kids to love school
- Help you get your kids to get excited about any *particular* subject, whether it's learning to spell or taking up trigonometry

Instead, we *do* promise to give you great advice that can:

- Help you stop worrying about your kids' grades and about their whole school performance.
- Help you get your kids excited about learning and become truly educated, in the biggest and best sense of the word.
- Help you, too, become a more lively, joyful, curious, growing human being.

We define an "educated" person as one whose inborn love of learning[1] is still intact (or has been reclaimed), and who chooses and has the skills to partake of the shared human creative endeavors of literature, science, and art. As a parent (Amy) and prospective parent (Grace), we want our children to be prepared to live life as creators: people who can act on what they imagine and make it real. The information children absorb and their exposure to our culture's intellectual history become most valuable when they deepen children's ability to participate richly in our civilization. Yes, "educated" people might get better-paying, more satisfying jobs than "uneducated" people. However, the real gift of a life in which one's love of learning is allowed to blossom is the possibility it provides to contribute and to enjoy the contributions of others.

We want to convince you of the futility of endlessly trying to force your children to comply with the often-arbitrary demands of school, to explain our views about how real learning happens, and mostly to show how all adults can support children in participating in our culture's shared creative conversation. We hope to inspire you to reinvent your *own* participation in that conversation, to assist your children in discovering their unique gifts and passions, and to replace the burden of endless worry and heartache about grades, homework,

---

[1] By the way, if you mentally substitute the word "life" every time we say "learning" or "education," you may understand more deeply what we're getting at. Unfortunately, our culture persists in seeing education or learning as a domain separate from the rest of life. If it didn't, we probably wouldn't need to write this book.

tests, and teachers' judgments with the joy of immediately beginning a life of learning, creating, and working diligently not for someone else's approval but for your own passion.

In other words, this book is an invitation. We invite you to consider possibilities. We believe that if you understand these possibilities, your relationship with your child's education will change, effortlessly and fluidly. We'll also preach at you a bit and give you "things to do"—this is a how-to book, after all. Mostly, though, we will again and again return to explain these new possibilities, and ask you to consider them. You'll probably find some of them counterintuitive—and ultimately you may even reject them as wrong or inappropriate, or inconsistent with your values. If you do, you'll have plenty of company among millions of other parents and teachers who support the educational status quo. But please think the possibilities through before you make such a choice.

This book applies to children from birth to eighteen; in other words, it applies to them as long as they're dependent on you, in school, or homeschooling under your jurisdiction. You'll need to use your common sense to adapt our suggestions if your children are at the older or younger extreme of the age range.

WHO WE ARE

Amy

I once wrote an article on homeschooling, which was published by a respected Boston-area alternative weekly. Out of the blue, an editor at a large New York publishing house contacted me, asking if I would be interested in writing a book on homeschooling. I said I wasn't. A literary agent then called me, asking if I was crazy to turn down an offer from a large publisher. I said many fine books on homeschooling had been published, that there was a limited audience for them (in my opinion), and that my habit of regularly buying these books and giving them to my "schooling" friends satisfied my need to proselytize about homeschooling.

As so often happens in life, one thing led to another. Eventually I decided I *would* be interested in writing a book (for which I found a coauthor—Grace is literally revered by much of the homeschooling community—and another publisher) that would introduce alternative education ideas to a mainstream audience. I wanted to write for the vast majority of American parents who might never buy or read books on homeschooling. Grace and I envisioned a book that would introduce to people who had kids in school, and were probably never going to take them out of school, some of the insights and discoveries born out of the ongoing cultural experiment that is homeschooling and alternative education.

I have helped raise two stepchildren and two foster children, all grown now. My own two children, Carsie and Elijah, are fifteen and seven at this writing. My kids have been homeschooled, private-schooled, and public-schooled. I've had kids labeled "learning-disabled," kids considered brilliant, early readers, and late readers. Most important, my community of friends and colleagues provides me with a knowledge base of the experiences of dozens of families, with hundreds of children, who have experimented with many different ways of raising and educating their kids. My two school-age children currently attend a small, cooperative, Waldorf-style school founded by families looking for alternatives in education. In addition to the stories of a number of other families who practice the kind of education we advocate, this book includes many "Carsie and Elijah" stories.

I have often been afraid, writing this book. I fear that sometimes our—Grace's and mine—attitudes toward school are too harsh and judgmental. I think of all the teachers I know who are kind and passionate, all the kids I know who are more or less happy in school. My father spent much of his adult life working for the U.S. Office (later Department) of Education, and thus I imagine that many or most education policymakers are thoughtful and goodhearted people. I certainly have no wish to criticize or judge parents who have their children in school. Yet I also have seen so many children gradually lose their enthusiasm, their openness, and their love of learning under the inexorable crush of school life. I saw it when I was a child, and I see it today. I have seen so many parents who are confused and anxious, torn between the unconditional love and compassion and support that they've been practicing since their children were born and their admirable desire to do the right thing once kids start school. I know that there are phalanxes of ambitious and idealistic school reformers out there, trying to change things in schools, just as there were when I went to school in the 1960s. They are the king's loyal opposition. They will always be with us.

I don't hate schools, and I have tried to keep the unkindness and harshness that sometimes creep into my tone out of this book. I know I have failed in places. Yet I write. I write with the hope that there are families out there who will be helped by our point of view, parents who might lighten up, kids who might not lose their self-confidence, maybe even teachers who will gain something from the stories we share. The college I attended had as its motto the Latin phrase "Facio liberos ex liberis libris libraque," which translates as "I make free adults out of children by means of books and a balance." It is with freedom, and its fundamental connection to education, that Grace and I are concerned as we write.

Grace

In public grade school, junior high, and high school, and then at the renowned private liberal arts college I attended, I warred with myself. I was bright and creative, loved to read and write, inherited from my family a strong belief in the importance of education. And so I thought that I should love school. But I didn't. Worse, no one offered to help me understand *why* I failed to love school or what I might do differently to make it work better for me. (Not that I thought to ask.) I alternated between blaming my teachers for being stupid or dull and blaming myself for being undisciplined or apathetic. Not that I complained much—like most kids, I complained some, but for the most part I just accepted my fate: This is the way things are. *The hours drag by, summer vacation is far away, I haven't done my algebra homework for a week and can't possibly catch up, this grammar worksheet looks like the same one we did last year and the year before, I know I should be excited about choosing a subject for my term paper but I'm not, I stare out the window a lot, sometimes I fall asleep in class. It's always been this way. It will always be this way.*

At the time it didn't occur to me to imagine that something could be different for *me*; I unconsciously imagined myself a victim of my circumstances. It did, however, occur to me to imagine other classes and teachers that were livelier, and I set out to "make it so," by becoming a teacher myself. I worked first as a public school substitute of everything from physics to choir, preschool through twelfth grade. Then I landed a dream job as a middle school language arts teacher in a small, creative, college prep school with a great reputation. But once part of the system—a giver-of-orders rather than a taker-of-orders—I found that the situation wasn't as simple as I'd imagined, and I began to see things more broadly. Even in the outstanding private school I worked for, various complications got in the way of my simply helping kids to learn. The class period would end just when we were really getting on a roll. Conversely, kids would come into my class with their heads still engaged in a science experiment or an argument with a friend. In an independent study program I designed, some students wanted to take on projects that didn't fit squarely enough within the realm of "language arts," so rather than cheer them on, I had to curtail and rein them in. Furthermore, the students took standardized tests each spring, so even though we were not supposed to "teach to the tests," we *were* supposed to have classes that tested well.

I knocked myself out designing and delivering lesson plans I hoped would be inspiring. Sure enough, a handful of my students raved about my classes, and some even wrote odes and unsolicited essays on my behalf. But on most days, the majority of my kids looked at me slack-jawed and stone-faced—until their lunch break, when they perked up, moved with grace and energy, spoke and laughed with animation.

I felt both reassured and further depressed by the fact that it obviously wasn't just me: My colleagues were some of the most brilliant and passionate people I've met, ever. Their students, too, looked for the most part slack-jawed and stone-faced. And in the public schools where I'd subbed, it had been worse. I read voraciously, to make sense of the situation, and John Holt's books changed my world. Through dozens of detailed personal anecdotes and warmly, clearly outlined logic, Holt convinced me to turn my view of education upside down:

> I can sum up in five to seven words what I eventually learned as a teacher. The seven-word version is: Learning is not the product of teaching. The five-word version is: Teaching does not make learning. . . . organized education operates on the assumption that children learn only when and only what and only because we teach them. This is not true. It is very close to one hundred percent false. Learners make learning. Learners create learning. The reason that this has been forgotten is that the activity of learning has been made into a product called "education," just as the activity, the discipline, of caring for one's health has become the product of "medical care," and the activity of inquiring into the world has become the product of "science," a specialized thing presumably done only by people with billions of dollars of complicated apparatus. But health is not a product and science is something you and I do every day of our lives.[2]

I field-tested Holt's ideas in my classrooms for a while, decided he was right as rain, and soon decided to take a whole new approach to teaching: I quit my job and wrote a book for teenagers telling them how, as the subtitle says, to "quit school and get a real life and education." For the ensuing ten years, I've worked in the midst of the "unschooling" wing of the homeschooling movement: recommending and selling books, speaking at conferences, directing a resource center, editing two books of autobiographical essays, running a summer camp for teenagers, reading and answering thousands of letters from my readers. I love this work. It gives me chills. I find it deeply

---

[2] From *Learning All the Time*, by John Holt (Cambridge, MA: Perseus, 1989).

rewarding and feel that I am able to empower people much more than I ever did, or could, by working in the school system. But . . .

I now live in the same city where I began my career as a substitute teacher, across the street from Laurel Grade School. My friends include two kindergartners, Jerome and Anita, who pick me beautiful bouquets of weeds and flowers and who ride their bikes up and down my street, and who eagerly tell me the words they can spell. I love their sweet, enthusiastic company, but I am afraid for them. When I subbed at Laurel and the other schools in this town, thirteen years ago, I mourned the awful contrast between the soft, eager eyes of the little kids and the hard, bitter eyes of the high school seniors. I know that school isn't the only factor in that terrible loss-of-self-esteem coming-of-age trend, but based on my work of the last thirteen years I am convinced it's one of the biggest factors. That way kids' eyes change, over time, had a lot to do with why I quit teaching and started advocating homeschooling and doing what I could to support homeschooling. But are Jerome and Anita going to homeschool? I doubt it. I imagine that they and about 95 percent of the other kids at Laurel, and at all the other schools in the United States, are never going to know the luxury or the expansive calm joy or the thrill of what we call "unschooling." (When you get down to it, unschooling is really just a fancy term for "life" or "growing up uninstitutionalized.") Not because their parents wouldn't make perfectly good homeschooling parents, but because homeschooling is still a misunderstood, largely unknown, even stigmatized alternative. And also because, although all kinds of families find ways to make homeschooling work for them—despite conflicts with careers, despite having little money—homeschooling *is* a big undertaking, particularly for families with young children.

And so I yearn to reach out to these kids, the kids at Laurel Grade School, which doesn't even have any grass for them to play on, by telling their parents—and all school parents—what I've learned from the homeschooling movement: *how they can reclaim their own power to help their kids blossom, no matter what kind of school experience they had or their children are having.*

Yes, "yearning" is the word that comes to mind. The unnamed yearning I felt as a kid and my yearning now to address the unspoken yearnings of kids and their parents: *There must be something more.* Of course, a different approach to education can't, in itself, fill all our deep bittersweet longings. But it's as good a place as any to start, and for many people—myself included—it's a giant step on the path to happier, more engaged, more generous living.

As I've worked with homeschoolers, I've continued to think more about my own school career—as both a student and a teacher. My interest now is broader than either schooling *or* homeschooling—it's about learning and growing: How can we, as adults, support kids in becoming their biggest, best, brightest selves? And—just as important—how can we, too, shed the straitjackets, fears, misconceptions, and heavy burdens that we picked up along the way and instead grow into our own shining possibilities? I am excited to tackle these questions in this book with Amy—whom I greatly admire both as a constantly growing individual and as a Guerrilla Learning parent—and with the insight and help of pioneering families who are living examples of what's possible for the rest of us.

How Did We Come Up with Guerrilla Learning?

By teaching school, watching students, and watching teachers. By raising children, teaching parenting classes, reflecting on our childhoods, watching parents, and watching ourselves. By reading educational philosophy. By talking to our friends and family about how we best learned and how we continue to learn.

We also got a lot of our ideas by homeschooling, observing and working with homeschoolers, reading homeschooling magazines and books, talking with and reading letters from thousands of homeschoolers . . . and in all of this, noticing what works and what doesn't work for them. That's not because we think Guerrilla Learning is possible only for homeschoolers; rather, it's because homeschoolers are a fantastic source of information. They try all kinds of things that most schools don't try (such as letting kids wait to start reading until they're ten years old, if they're not ready earlier, or letting kids focus whole-heartedly on their favorite subject). Then the rest of us get to benefit from the results of their experiments.

Finally, we interviewed several dozen families from all over the country and from all walks of life whom we feel exemplify the possi-bilities expressed in this book. Although some of them have experi-mented with homeschooling, these families all have kids in school, most of them in traditional schools. In one way, this book is our attempt to let these people, who have experimented with education in ways that are nontraditional and yet within reach for families who can't or don't want to homeschool, speak directly to a wider audi-ence. We tell their stories here.

You may notice that a disproportionate number of the parents in our Guerrilla Learning families, as we call them, are teachers. We believe that the reason so many teachers responded to our call for family stories is that they know firsthand what actually goes on inside public school classrooms. Therefore, they are less likely than other adults to unquestioningly accept school authorities' interpretations of events and more likely to search for alternative ways to support their children's learning.

WHAT THIS BOOK IS NOT

We haven't written a book about school reform. There are many such books, written by brilliant and dedicated people. Often their ideas are based on the same research and thinking that we discuss here. Instead, this book is about what *families* can do, rather than sit around waiting for the schools to reform themselves.

Nor is this a book about how to "bring school home" by inserting schoollike activities into more of your child's waking hours. Plenty of other books suggest ways to turn all of life into a series of academic lessons. For example, you can teach fractions while baking cherry pie, show alphabet flash cards to babies, or transform every car trip into a history lesson. While we don't always object to these kinds of activities per se, we think that approach is often overdone and misguided. (In any case, it's not our interest here.) We will focus not on how parents can teach their children in order to reinforce or supplement the school agenda but on how parents can allow their children to do what they are hungry, ready, and willing to do from the day they're born: *learn*.

1
The Broken Sword

Real Education in Our Lives
and the Lives of Our Children

o—⚷

To be prepared against surprise is to be *trained*.
To be prepared for surprise is to be *educated*.

—James P. Carse,
Finite and Infinite Games

This is a book for parents who have kids in school. It's partly based, though, on things we discovered about kids who *weren't* in the traditional school system. Let's begin by sharing some of those discoveries.

People who were in the midst of the homeschooling movement of the 1980s and 1990s noticed a curious thing: that homeschooled kids—many of whom did few or no traditional, "schoollike" activities at home—learned faster, more easily, and with more joy and enthusiasm than most other children. They remembered what they learned. They couldn't wait to learn more.

Even those kids whose parents mimicked school's subject divisions, worksheets, and memorization-regurgitation loops learned so quickly and so easily that their lives focused more on the fun and interesting projects they devised to fill their free time than on their "schoolwork."

Most of the homeschoolers—the kids in freer, "unschooling" homes as well as those doing more traditional "school-at-home"— were engaged in ambitious, serious projects of one kind or another:

raising lambs, competing in geography bees, creating businesses, publishing newsletters, painting murals. In addition to their academic progress, they were learning the critical skills needed to devise a project, commit to a goal, and, at the risk of real failure, make something happen in the world.

Critics of homeschooling warned that these kids wouldn't measure up academically. When test scores silenced their objections (since they tended to be the kind of people who believe that test scores measure learning), the critics started worrying about "socialization," something that was hypothetically taking place in school classrooms. Those worries also proved unfounded, but we'll leave that question aside. What we're interested in here is why learning seems to be so much easier at *home*, even when approached casually, than in a formal academic environment. *Are there any principles at work in this situation that parents who have kids in school can learn, apply, and use to their advantage?*

LEARNING REQUIRES MEANING

Here is what we think lies behind the mysterious power of homeschooling: *Real learning requires meaning.* Meaningless information can be memorized and repeated, but that's not learning. It's more like programming, or what writer Joseph Chilton Pearce calls "conditioning."

For information to have meaning, there must be a meaningful *context* for the information. Information without a context is not actually information at all but data. For example, a computer stores data, but it doesn't *understand* the data. For the data to become information, a human being has to get involved.

In other words, when confronted with this question:

A plumber charges $35 to send a service person on a call and $20 per hour for labor. If n stands for the number of hours of labor, which expression below could a customer use to compute a charge for a service call?

. . . or this one:

Distinguish between the judicial systems established by the Virginia and United States Constitutions.[1]

. . . a student who fills in the right "bubble" has not necessarily *learned* anything at all. No meaningful context for this information is apparent to the child. (The pretense of phrasing the algebra question as if it applied to a "real-life" situation—a plumbing service—isn't going to fool any seventh grader into thinking the problem is relevant to anything in real experience.)

For real learning to take place, the information must occur in a *world*. For medical students, for example, the world in which learning occurs can be seen as the world of healing, the lab, and the hospital. For auto mechanics, it's the world of the garage. The relationship of the information to reality—its context—must be apparent. People can be asked to absorb a certain amount of meaningless data in good faith, on the promise that eventually it will be related to a larger world and transformed into information. But most people can't absorb meaningless data on good faith for twelve years.

"The first lesson I teach is confusion," says award-winning teacher John Taylor Gatto, in his ironic speech about the harmful "lessons" that all school teachers inevitably teach. (The speech was all the more ironic considering its occasion: Gatto's acceptance of the New York State Teacher of the Year Award in 1991.) In school, says Gatto, nearly everything is presented out of context, segregated and disconnected from everything else. Even the best curricula lack coherence and suffer internal contradictions. "Confusion is thrust upon kids by too many strange adults, each working alone with only the thinnest relationship with each other, pretending, for the most part, to an expertise they do not possess."[2]

If you think kids who perform well in school aren't confused, think again. Harvard researcher Howard Gardner describes experiments designed to reveal students' real-world knowledge of physics, as opposed to their ability to parrot correct answers on a test. Under

---

[1] Required knowledge for all Virginia seventh graders according to Virginia's "Standards of Learning."

[2] Reprinted from John Taylor Gatto, *Dumbing Us Down: The Hidden Curriculum of Compulsory Schooling* (New York: New Society Publishers, 1991), p. 13.

these conditions, college physics students fall back on guesses like those offered by elementary school students. Gardner reports, "Researchers at John Hopkins, M.I.T., and other well-regarded universities have documented that students who receive honors grades in college-level physics courses are frequently unable to solve basic problems and questions encountered in a form slightly different from that on which they have been formally instructed and tested." The students' schooling, at which they excelled, failed to change their naïve, intuitive—but wrong—attitudes at all.[3]

When Amy's daughter Carsie was eight, she attended an environmental summer camp on North Carolina's Outer Banks. One of the staff naturalists happened to come across Carsie kneeling on the boardwalk alongside the preserve building, watching a small reptile crawl out of a hole in the wood. "Find a lizard?" asked the naturalist. "Actually, I think it's a skink," replied the eight-year-old. To Amy, who was watching (proudly, she admits), the naturalist looked surprised that a child knew the difference. It's the kind of academic information that kids usually don't get so early. But Carsie hadn't learned it in school—she'd learned it by spending her days exploring the woods and fields near her house, catching critters, looking them up in books, and discussing them with her friends. A friend of her father's, a zookeeper, had taught her how to make a lizard-catcher out of a stick, a paper clip, a cotton ball, and some dental floss. She knew what different kinds of lizards ate and how you catch or grow their prey. The distinction "skink" didn't belong in a classroom or a textbook to her, it belonged in her world. (At that age Carsie could also explain fairly thoroughly the difference between reptiles and amphibians and what distinguishes them both from mammals—all information that had its source in her "field-based" work.)

---

[3] Howard Gardner, *The Unschooled Mind: How Children Think & How Schools Should Teach* (New York: Basic Books, 1991), p. 3.

WHAT IS A CHILD'S WORLD?

On the other hand, a homeschooled child learns everything in a meaningful context. The context is automatic: It's *the child's world.* For children, at least until adolescence, the world is mostly the realm of home and family.

Advocates of "natural" or "interest-led" learning sometimes talk about "using the world as the classroom." *Take those kids out of the classroom and into the real world, and they'll learn better!* say these progressive educators. And we agree: Kids *do* learn better in the real world. However, we think the phrase "the world as the classroom" is misleading. The world doesn't need to be a classroom—it's the *world!* Things we learn in and about the real world make sense, fit naturally into our emerging model of reality, and relate to each other in obvious ways. It's not that the world is a good classroom; it's that classrooms are poor worlds. Classroom-acquired data won't necessarily make the shift into authentic information. That's why most people, unless they happen to be really good at absorbing and retaining meaningless data, forget most of what they learn in school.

Children—all of us, actually—are always forming a mental model of the world and trying to fit new information into it. Sometimes the whole model has to be revised, as in adolescence when a crisis of meaning may lead a young person to adopt an entirely new ideology. What works so powerfully for homeschooled kids is that they are naturally gathering new information all the time and fitting it into their developing mind-model. They are constantly studying the world around them—the social world, the physical world, and the cultural world—and asking questions about it to plug the holes in their model. Each new bit of data, often presented in the form of the answer to a question, tends to fit right in. In fact, children's questions are the most critical clue to what information is currently required by their emerging internal map of the world. That's why allowing children to follow their interests can make learning so powerful. Kids' interests are often the clues to what's missing in their mind-models.

One reason that a child's home is such a natural place for learning is that home, unlike school, is never general or homogeneous. The very word "home" implies something personal, something particular, and somewhere one *exclusively* belongs. Home is always a specific place, at a specific time, with these specific people. It *matters* where you live, who your family is, what history and culture grew you. Children can't create a mental model of the entire world that includes all cultures, all of physical reality, and all of history. They have to start *someplace.* Homeschoolers in the Shenandoah Valley of Virginia, for example (where Amy and her family live), in addition to learning about skinks, tend to study the Civil War and visit Civil War battlefields. They might explore the Shenandoah River—why is it one of the only rivers in America that flows north?—and follow it to its confluence with the Potomac River, at Harper's Ferry, and then to the Chesapeake Bay, learning what an estuary is and who John Brown was along the way. Homeschoolers in the nearby city of Washington, D. C., might spend more time at art museums and in libraries and at poetry slams. They might be aware of politics at an earlier age. Homeschoolers understand and retain what they learn because the relationship between the information and the world—their world—is so transparent. Even when homeschooling parents do act like traditional teachers, they tend to relate information to the child's world naturally and automatically. They know their children, and their children's world, so well that they can't help it.

Schools Decontextualize Information

In contrast, unfortunately, most schools work on the opposite assumption. They remove information from its context. They present a parade of decontextualized data, year after year, that bears little or no relationship to the child's world beyond the abstract world of the classroom. Subjects are artificially separated from one another. It's as if schools believe that if you give kids one tree at a time, year after year after dreary year, the kids will save the trees up and eventually make a forest out of them.

Think about what the expression "it's academic" means: that the point you're arguing has no bearing on anything real or essential.

Some educators—called Progressives—have tried to bring more of the real world into the classroom. Progressives pay attention to child development and learning research that has repeatedly shown that people learn better when they're interested, when the context is meaningful, and when they're ready. But currently progressive education is in disfavor, and traditional, decontextualized, reality-free schooling is enjoying a huge resurgence in the "Standards" movement. Its proponents disregard research on learning and emphasize "high-stakes testing," a method that often ends up with kids simply working to memorize fact collections. The movement has led to the repeal of recess in many schools (beginning in kindergarten) and, in some states, to the doubling of average homework loads. Many talented teachers have resigned as a result, rather than lose autonomy in the classroom and become mere test coaches.

Yet test scores and grades don't actually predict anything much. (Can you imagine if kids *knew* that secret?!) Higher-level skills such as critical thinking are neither taught nor tested in most schools. Artistic ability, mechanical ingenuity, interpersonal strengths, musical talent, and gifts for synthesizing information are disregarded (if not disparaged). People who can quickly memorize meaningless data and deliver it on demand are rewarded, while poor test takers with other strengths are penalized. Unlike in life, the compliant are favored over the willful. And the greatest opportunity of childhood—the opportunity children have to develop their strengths, cultivate self-discipline, and find their *calling*—is ignored in favor of the effort to teach what can be measured.

So we'll say it, even though it may be obvious: Academic success is *not* necessarily success in life. Nor is it necessarily education. It's a narrow kind of performance, with narrow effects. And if success in life is becoming more dependent on academic achievement because new hoops are being set up through which kids must jump before they're allowed to go to college, or to qualify for financial aid, we need to understand why this is so, who made it so, and whether it's in our children's best interests or not.

Given That Your Kids Go to School . . .

We'll offer you two kinds of advice:
1. How to help your kids deal with school;

2. How to help your kids educate themselves—not in school specifically, but in life.

We'll offer you tips and information that can help kids get better at traditional kinds of school performance. For example, we'll discuss learning styles and direct you to resources that can help you teach your kids to use their strengths instead of endlessly trying to overcome their weaknesses. We'll discuss alternatives to traditional school and direct you to resources about these alternatives. We'll also advise as much as possible doing an "end run" around schools and their sometimes absurd requirements that usurp more and more of children's time and attention without really educating them. Finally, we'll caution you to pay attention to the emotional consequences of school's demands.

You see, there *are* costs to school's often-absurd requirements—costs that we once took for granted, since school seemed inevitable. We ourselves began questioning the inevitability of school's costs only when we saw that there were real, effective alternatives and real ways to protect kids who are in school from school's potential damage.

School can sap kids' interest in learning, confuse them with so many meaningless "trees" that it takes years for them to recover and begin to see the "forest" again. School can simply eat up so much of their time that there's none left for real learning, for spontaneous exploration, or for free play, which is the real work of childhood. At worst, school can cause true emotional stress: anxiety, depression, and crippling self-doubt. Instead of discovering their unique gifts, talents, and place in the world, many kids will learn to see themselves as mediocre, as "disabled," or as losers if they don't keep up with the traditional school system's standards of measurement. Even the "winners" may one day awaken to wonder why they spent their youths chasing after external approval, meaningless incentives, and other people's purposes—"gold stars"—to the exclusion of what they loved and cared about.

WHERE EDUCATION *REALLY* HAPPENS

For the most part our kids will survive, and things will go on as they always have: With certain exceptions, the children of educated people will be educated and the children of educationally deprived people will stay educationally deprived. Why? Is it because the schools of educated people have so much more money? Maybe. Most of the educational establishment, and certainly most politicians, would like us all to believe that money equals education. John Gatto has made convincing arguments against the money equals education theory, however, pointing out that before compulsory schooling in America,

---

During the autumn of 2000, while she spends her days finishing the writing of *Guerrilla Learning*, Amy is reading Tolkien's *The Fellowship of the Ring* to Elijah, who is seven and a half, at bedtime. At this writing they're on page 356—it's by far the longest book they've ever read together. (They haven't tackled the *Harry Potter* series yet.) It's also the most fun for Amy to read. She's invented accents for all the different characters. (Although she has no particular talent for accents, Elijah is still too young to criticize her attempts.) Elijah, who is a strongly kinesthetic learner, has a tendency to jump up in the middle of a passage and act out a scene.

One recent morning Elijah approached Amy and presented a life-size sword he had made out of Lego blocks.

"It's the broken sword," said Elijah (refererring to a sword mentioned in the Tolkien classic).

"Oh! Aragorn's sword?" asked Amy.

"Yep! I can fix it, and then I'm a smith!" said Elijah. He had designed the sword in two pieces so that you could "mend" it by pressing the two parts together.

"Didn't the sword have a name?" Amy asked.

Elijah thought for a few moments. "I can't remember. I'll get the book!" He brought the book to Amy and she leafed through it.

"Aragorn took his sword with him when they left Rivendell," Elijah reminded her.

"Okay, I'll find that part," said Amy. "Here it is . . . Andúril!"

"That's right," said Elijah, happily repeating the word and waving the sword. "*Andúril.*"

the unschooled, mostly farming population was more literate and better educated than afterward.[4]

Maybe things go on the way they do because, at least until college, much of real learning doesn't even happen in school. It happens *at home.* It happens when children are read bedtime stories, and in dinner-table conversations, and on family vacations. It happens in the thousands of small interactions between the child and the immediate and extended family. *We're all "homeschooling," all the time.*

Here is what we believe the "broken sword" incident taught, or reinforced for, Elijah: Literature is a rich, satisfying, natural part of life. It brings joy to adults and children. And long stories that require sustained attention over time can be particularly rewarding. We can be a part of the richness of literature through dramatization, through sharing it with each other, and through creating our own crafts or art that reference the stories we love. We try to remember what we have read as a way of keeping the richness in our lives. And if we can't remember things, we look them up.

School vs. Education

School is not education. School is an institution devised by social engineers who had certain specific aims in addition to education. One of their goals was to remove all children from their homes and instill them with a homogeneous, shared American culture. Over the 150 or so years since compulsory schooling became universal in this country, school has changed, of course, but has not strayed terribly far from its origins in social control.

"Universal schooling in America was introduced, in part, to prepare children for new ways of living and working that were a consequence of industrialization," writes David Elkind in his 1984 book, *The Hurried Child.* Elkind discusses the stress and suffering produced by today's pressure on kids to grow up faster and faster. He explains how our schools are designed on a "factory" model, in which teachers are

---

[4] See John Taylor Gatto's *The Underground History of American Education* (New York: Oxford Village Press, 2000). See also Frank Smith, *The Book of Learning and Forgetting* (New York: Teacher's College Press, 1998).

viewed as "workers" and children as "products." "[School] administrators are under stress to produce better 'products.' This blinds them to what we know about children and leads them to treat children like empty bottles on an assembly line getting a little fuller at each grade level. . . . This factory emphasis . . . ignores individual differences in mental ability and learning rates."[5]

Our schools are out of sync with the larger society, claims Elkind, and represent the past, not the future. Not only do they treat education as if it could be divided, broken down, and homogenized on the industrial model, schools also are designed to prepare children for life in an industrial society—a society where a central, controlling elite manages the lives of the population. As John Gatto says, "Schools were designed . . . to be instruments of the scientific management of a mass population. . . . to produce, through the application of formulas, formulaic human beings whose behavior can be predicted and controlled."[6] American schools were deliberately modeled on Prussian schools of the mid-nineteenth century, according to Gatto, the purpose of which was:

> . . . not intellectual development at all, but socialization in obedience and subordination. Thinking was left to the Real Schulen [Real Schools], in which 8% of the kids participated. But for the great mass, intellectual development was regarded with managerial horror, as something that caused armies to lose battles. For Prussia the ideal model society was not intellectual Greece or muscular Rome but solid, settled Egypt—a pyramid of subordination where only the top leadership understood the big picture. Below this class were descending service classes, each larger than the one directly above it, each knowing less than the one above it until at the bottom almost nothing was known except how to do a small part of a larger task only dimly understood.[7]

---

[5] David Elkind, *The Hurried Child: Growing Up Too Fast Too Soon* (New York: Knopf, 1984), p. 48.

[6] Gatto, *Dumbing Us Down*, p. 57.

[7] John Taylor Gatto, keynote speech to the Conference on Private Initiatives in Education, Indianapolis, Indiana, November 13–14, 1992.

Real education, in contrast, prepares one to think critically and comprehensively, argue effectively, and find one's singular, irreplaceable calling in life and the skills to pursue it. It prepares us for self-reliance, not for dependency on others' approval, on social institutions, or on ready-made ideologies. Gatto and others believe that forced, systematic, government-monopoly schooling was a conscious attempt to interfere with the thriving American experiment of self-reliance and individuality.

Whatever the Reasons, Schools Are the Way They Are— and We Can Stop Pretending They're Otherwise

Perhaps no one deliberately aimed to design schools that would leave most of the people in them—teachers as well as children—uninspired, cynical, and defeated. Perhaps our schools are only victims of the trap into which all human institutions, as mythologist Joseph Campbell has pointed out, fall prey: They evolve into systems with their own purposes and ultimately come to exist for the preservation of their own survival, rather than to serve the human beings whose lives they were originally designed to enhance.

Thus government officials wind up working for the expansion of their departments, instead of for the improvement of public life; healthcare systems shift paradoxically toward conditions hostile to health; and religious institutions can grow, in time, to be the least likely places on earth one might experience the divine.

Systems by their nature are unfeeling, rigid, and abstract. They take what is alive and turn it into machinery, sacrificing vitality for efficiency. One function of mythology, said Campbell, is to help people transform and transcend outmoded systems, which have inevitably grown self-serving and gained a stranglehold on the life of the community.

No matter what caused our schools to be the way they are, if one looks honestly and openly at them—now and in the past—cynicism and defeat is what one sees. But often we don't look honestly and openly. As parents, as teachers, as grown-up children ourselves, we often ignore our real-world experience of schools in favor of a shared cultural fiction about how school works. We've been subtly indoctrinated into a fable that somewhere there exists a peaceful, orderly classroom, full of happy, diligent children, where the strict but loving teacher inspires young minds to love learning and to develop discipline. But this classroom almost never appears here and now. Where is this ideal classroom? It is down the hall. No. . . . Then it must be in another school, across town, or across the country. Wait, that was several years ago. Oh, you went to that school? It wasn't like that, after all? Did this ideal school exist in the 1950s, or was it in the late nineteenth century?

If our children would just buckle down, implies the cultural myth, or parents were more involved, or teachers were better trained, or the newest ideas and techniques were implemented, or we returned to the basic techniques of the past, our classrooms would work too.

Maybe some people experienced such a classroom in their youth. Or maybe some kids are in one right now. For many, however, the ideal-school myth distracts us from noticing the actual conditions of *this* school, *these* children, the reality in which we live. Like unattainable ideals about family life, this ideal is not inspiring but oppressive. It doesn't tell us *how* to be the way these ideal people are; it just tells us that the way we are is wrong. The unattainable ideal distracts us with an inappropriate question: *What's wrong?* What's wrong with my kids? What's wrong with this classroom? This school? This teacher? Kids these days? The country? Me?

RECLAIMING OUR RESPONSIBILITY FOR EDUCATION

While policymakers, politicians, and experts argue over what's wrong, parents, children, and even teachers are seldom asked what they *want.* Sometimes parents take matters into their own hands, assuming they have the time and resources to do so, and change schools, homeschool, even start new schools. The vast majority (90 percent—about 45 million as of this writing) of American children, however, continue their daily march to the local public school. And the vast majority of these schools operate on the traditional, authoritarian, no-context model: trees now, forest later. Even where other models are valued, the traditional model—based on the conviction that children do not want to learn and must be forced to learn the correct material at the proper time—often has a deep, though subtle, influence.

We invite you to discard the oppressive ideal of the "perfect" classroom—whether traditional or progressive—because that ideal subtly robs families of their own power and responsibility. We say that *education is the responsibility (and privilege) of the family*, regardless of current laws and social structures and economic needs. Sending children to school does not relieve the family of that responsibility. Instead of asking, "What would make schools better?" or "How can we get our kids to perform better in school?" this book invites you to ask "What is education to our family?"—to ask what kind of lives you want for your children and what kind of lives they want for themselves.

Like you, we, the authors, struggle with the question of how to raise and educate kids. In fact, we see ourselves partly as correspondents from the front, sharing stories about people who have created their own solutions to the problem of school. People who have attempted to preserve their children's aliveness, freedom, and humanity, despite their awareness that the institution in which children spend their days seems calculated, at times, to crush their spirits. Who, while taking full advantage of the benefits and resources that schools offer, still have the audacity to demand that children make their own choices, control their own lives, and retain authority over their own souls. This book is not about what's wrong that needs fixing but about *what's possible that calls to be celebrated.*

You can view school as a deadly serious, meaningful test of who your family and your child really are and the only significant source of children's learning. (That's how many of the people who run schools, fund schools, and worry about schools would like you to view it.) Or you can choose to look at school as a game, with certain rules, certain penalties for losing and rewards for winning, and certain costs of playing. It doesn't have to define who your child or your family are. It doesn't have to be the only, or even the main, source of your child's education. It probably won't much help your children find and develop their strengths (unless their strengths happen to be primarily academic), grow as whole, healthy, spiritually connected, intellectually vital people, or find their calling in life. *But neither does it have to crush their spirits.*

Confusing the Means with the Ends

Once upon a time a man asked his wife why she always cut off both ends of a ham before she baked it. "It's just the right way to do it," she replied, "My mother taught me." Dissatisfied, the man questioned his mother-in-law at the next gathering. "Everybody cooks ham that way," she answered, "My mother showed me when I was young." The grand-mother-in-law was still alive, and the husband, now very curious, called her. "Why do you cut off both ends of a ham before you cook it?" "I only had one pan, and the ham wouldn't fit unless I cut off the ends," replied the old woman.

It seems to us that much of what goes on in schools is like this fam-ily's ham-trimming custom. People do it because they've always done it that way, or it once had a purpose, or it has a purpose that is fun-damentally unrelated to the larger professed goal of the schools, in the same way that the pan size is unrelated to the goal of cooking a ham. The ends have become the means, as it were. There's nothing

Chapter One: The Broken Sword

EXERCISES

These exercises, like those in the rest of the book, are not required, there are no right or wrong answers, and, of course, you won't be graded or tested on them. Do them if you choose. They may help you discover new ways of thinking about school.

"THE BEGINNER'S GUIDE . . . "

List everything about which you know enough to contribute signifi-cantly to a conversation on the subject or to write a pithy booklet called "The Beginner's Guide to _____."

Now write down everything you're good at—all your skills, any-thing from designing Web pages, to changing a diaper, to writing a newspaper story, to building a fence.

Now take a moment to consider whether your lists are longer or shorter than you would have expected. (Or ask several people who have very different school backgrounds from you to make their own lists, and compare the length and quality of your lists to theirs.)

Next, put an asterisk by each of the items that you learned mainly in school or college.

Finally, consider what percentage of your skills and expertise you've picked up in school and what outside of school.

THE WAY WE WERE

Take a moment to recall your experience of school. Cast your memory back, for a moment, to those years. Close your eyes if it helps. Allow the feelings, the sounds, the texture of your early grades, your middle school, your high school to emerge. The noise in the halls. The scarred desktops. Opening a textbook. Listening to a teacher lecture, scold, or praise. Lunch. Recess. Was there a particular teacher you loved? One you hated? Feared? One whom you believed hated you? A teacher you disliked then but admire now? Remember taking a test? Watching the clock? Trying to finish your homework? Did you ever finish your homework and then lose it? Did you work hard at an assignment and fail, or hardly work on it and succeed?

Remember the last day of school before summer vacation? The last day of summer vacation?

Finally, recall your social experience of school. Who were your friends? Were there kids you didn't like or who didn't like you? Did it change over the years? Did you feel accepted or excluded? Did you confide in your parents or other adults? Did you feel that you got help when you needed it?

---

wrong with cutting off the ends of the ham, of course (except waste, and maybe it dries out a bit). It's just that when you pretend you're cutting those ends off for some purpose other than efficiency, you stop yourself from seeing other possibilities.

In the case of children and school, pretending that the means are the same as the ends—that schooling is the same as education—actually can obscure the ends. Kids can grow up thinking that they don't really want education, or that they're no good at it, or that they *have* it, when all they don't want, or are no good at, or have is *schooling*.

"Wait a minute!" we imagine readers saying, "You're out of control! Isn't there *anything* good about schools?"

Of course there is. Schools have libraries, gyms, pianos, soccer fields, locker rooms, darkrooms, balance beams, Bunsen burners, and computers. Most have half a dozen or more inspired and inspiring teachers as well as many other kind, caring, friendly adults. But as a culture, we tend to assume that schools are basically a good system, with only cosmetic or surface-level problems. It's high time we turned our thinking upside down and recognized this antiquated institution for what it is. Once we recognize the danger, we will be much better able to negotiate our way through it—not just surviving it but actually *using* it. Like many other things in life, school can be a poor master but a good servant. As flawed as school is, it still wouldn't be such a problem if parents and kids didn't perceive it as the only source of learning and the final authority on education.

Part of the way we can deflect school's damaging ideology is by establishing our own larger and more powerful definition of education. Then we can avail ourselves of the advantages of twenty-first-century schools; indeed, we can almost treat them as resource centers, albeit with some annoying inconveniences and a steep price tag (mainly in the form of *time* unnecessarily spent on busywork) but with no power to do significant harm to our children. But we're getting ahead of ourselves. That's what the rest of this book is all about.

Resources

Elkind, David. *The Hurried Child: Growing Up Too Fast Too Soon.* New York: Knopf, 1984.

Gardner, Howard. *The Unschooled Mind: How Children Think & How Schools Should Teach.* New York: Basic Books, 1991.

Gatto, John Taylor. *Dumbing Us Down: The Hidden Curriculum of Compulsory Schooling.* New York: New Society Publishers, 1991.

Holt, John. *Freedom and Beyond.* Portsmouth, NH: Heinemann, 1972, 1995.

Kohn, Alfie. *Punished by Rewards: The Trouble with Gold Stars, Incentive Plans, A's, Praise, and Other Bribes.* New York: Houghton Mifflin, 1993.

2
What We Can Do
Guerrilla Learning

Bit by bit, I began to devise guerrilla exercises to allow the kids I
taught—as many as I was able—the raw material people have always
used to educate themselves: privacy, choice, freedom from surveillance,
and as broad a range of situations and human associations as my limited
power and resources could manage. In simpler terms, I tried to maneuver
them into positions where they would have a chance to be their own
teachers and to make themselves the major text of their own education.
—John Taylor Gatto, *Dumbing Us Down*.

guerrilla [gə 'ri-lə] n. [Sp, dim. of *guerra*, war] a member of a small
defensive force of irregular soldiers, making surprise raids.

We swiped John Gatto's "guerrilla" metaphor for the title of this book,
albeit our slight reservations about using a military metaphor. While
we are not generally in favor of war, we liked the "guerrilla" image of
a nimble, zealous, loosely organized group of kids educating themselves "beneath the radar" of the dominant school paradigm. The
power of guerrilla forces lies in their passion and flexibility. Dedica-
tion to a shared vision of freedom allows guerrillas to resist much bigger, better-funded, and better-organized forces.

Guerrilla Learning is coloring outside the lines, finding the short-
est direction between two points, moving directly toward goals, doing
the best you can with what you've got to work with now, making what
you want for your kids and what they want for themselves as real as you

can, asking people for specific kinds of help, getting out of theory land and into the trenches, realizing that schools could take centuries to significantly improve (or to get out of the way altogether) and that meanwhile your children are barreling through childhood.

Guerrilla Learning is letting your daughter read her stack of library books instead of finishing her homework. It's hiring your son's beloved third-grade teacher to give him written feedback on his poetry, even though now he's eleven years old. It's inviting your massage therapist to dinner, since your daughter's been talking about going to massage school instead of college—even if the thought worries you a little. It's telling your daughter *how* that thought worries you and listening to her talk about her motives. It might even be supporting your son's dropping out of college and investing his savings in his new Internet business instead—knowing the risk that involves and knowing your son might not fully appreciate the risk.

Guerrilla Learning is committing to learn Spanish fluently, as you've always planned to do, and attending a church where the service is in Spanish as well as listening to audiotapes. It's going back and reading Shakespeare, now that you don't have to and now that you've lived a little more and you can appreciate his wisdom. It's going to a lecture on evolution, which leads you to read Jared Diamond's *The Third Chimpanzee*, which leads you to the zoo, with or without your kids. It's volunteering in the ticket booth at a community-based dance series, so that you and your family can attend for free. It's reading and writing and building and enterprising and listening to music and doing and discussing all these things with your kids. It's continuously reawakening your own intellectual vitality (or rediscovering it, if you've misplaced it) and sharing it with your children.

Guerrilla Learning is telling your son it's okay for him to focus on physics (or history, or engine repair) class, even if that means letting history (or physics, or engine repair) slide. It's staying up till midnight helping your kids care for an orphaned bird. It's asking your neighbors if they'd let your daughter play their piano a few hours each week. It's telling your stressed-out son that there's no rush; he doesn't need to start college right after graduating from high school (or learn to read by the end of first grade, or keep up with his friends' computer expertise, or learn to drive next summer). Or allowing your sixteen-year-old daughter to start college now, if she feels she's ready. Or letting her ride her bicycle from Virginia to a summer camp in Oregon. It's trusting your kids, trusting the universe: The sky will not fall if your son doesn't take Advanced Placement courses or if your daughter doesn't belong to the National Honor Society. And Guerrilla Learning is relaxing—knowing that you've made a lot of mistakes as a parent (and an educator) and that you'll make a lot more, and that that's okay—your kids are resilient; it's not all up to you, and life will provide.

In a nutshell, Guerrilla Learning means taking responsibility for your own education. For young people, that includes thinking clearly and seriously about one's own goals, interests, and values—then acting accordingly. For parents, it means supporting your child in doing so. It might mean giving your child a kind of freedom that may seem risky or even crazy at first. And it also means continuing your own involvement in the world of ideas and culture, continuing to read, to think, to discuss, and to create—and being a walking, talking invitation to your kids to do the same. In this chapter we'll begin to describe conditions that can help learners to take responsibility for their own educations.

CONVENTIONAL FAMILIES AND GUERRILLA LEARNING FAMILIES

In the conventional family, one or both parents go to work, children go to school, and any hobbies or interests are pursued in spare time. Work is meaningful because it produces income; school is meaningful because it leads to work in the future. Hobbies are frivolous "extras" that one explores as a form of entertainment, to get one's mind off the serious, boring business of life. Parents leave the children's education up to the professionals whose work is teaching. The real job of parents when it comes to education is to discipline the children: making sure they attend school, behave when there, and do their homework.

If anything goes wrong—the child won't obey, won't or can't learn, or manifests troubling behavior—the parent's job is to step in and figure out what's wrong and what needs to happen (change schools, change programs, exert more discipline, bring in experts to diagnose learning disabilities) to fix the problem.

In this model, the child is more likely to be viewed as a passive recipient of certain "content"—facts, information, and ideas—and skills. Traditional education emphasizes fact-rich content such as dates and procedures; progressive education emphasizes "higher-order" skills such as critical thinking. Either way, school generally is viewed as a race, the purpose of which is preparation for the future economic race of life. There are winners and losers in life, and kids who do well in school can be winners. (Of course, for winning to be valuable, there *must* be losers—but that's another topic.)

In what we will call Guerrilla Learning families, in contrast, adults and children explore opportunities, set goals, and pursue their interests together. School is one resource among many for kids to use to develop their skills and understanding of the world. The end of formal schooling does not mean the end of learning but rather the beginning of an exciting new phase of discovery. Instead of a race with winners and losers, life is seen as a gift and learning—the wealth of human science and culture—one of its treasures. We don't learn in order to live; we live in order to learn.

A Guerrilla Learning family may explore different ways and styles of life in order to handle economic necessities without compromising its central values, such as time to spend together as a family. In addition to being models of creative, intellectually vital, contributing adults, parents act as guides and coaches for children, making sure they're exposed to a range of opportunities, helping them set and pursue goals, and being sensitive to their developmental stage and present needs as they grow. Self-reliance and critical thinking are often valued above obedience.

Of course, most of us fall into *both* of these categories in one way or another. They are artificial ideals, exaggerated to illustrate two distinct paradigms of how we might understand our lives. Yet some families tend more toward one extreme or the other. This chapter tells the stories of a few families who are plainly passionate Guerrilla Learners, who might be models for those readers who find them-

---

Susan and Michael Gushue (pronounced Goo-Shoo) and their five children, ages two through fifteen, live in a sprawling Victorian house in northeast Washington, D.C. Both graduates of St. John's College's classics-based "Great Books" program, Susan and Michael have thought long and hard about what education is, what kind of lives they want for their children, and what kind of family life they value. Michael is a government contracting officer and a published poet; Susan is a part-time math tutor and school reform activist. All their children have grown up attending D.C.'s public schools, although Charles, the oldest, was homeschooled during sixth, seventh, and eighth grades.

What dominates the Gushues' home, besides the ubiquitous presence of children of all sizes and activity levels, is books. Floor-to-ceiling bookcases line most of the rooms. Books are piled on tables and chairs. Fifteen-year-old Charles's bedroom door has a hanging rack of neatly arranged paperbacks on the back. Shelves overflow with children's books. The adults in the family collect books at Goodwill stores, estate and yard sales, and anywhere else good hardbacks can be had reasonably; however, the Gushues' books aren't bought just for their looks. Everyone in the family, except for two-year-old Nora, reads voraciously, constantly, and enthusiastically. And even Nora spends her time surrounded by people of all ages who discuss books and ideas with joy and passion.

"An educated person is curious," says Susan. "The more you know, the more there is for you to be curious about. So, it's just this constant thing—you learn, and then you get curious about even more things, and there are more questions you have.

"Helen, our eleven-year-old—it's so beautiful to watch her," Susan continues. "She's really into birds and music. She listens to all kinds of music, and she plays the sax, the piano, and the violin. This year she got interested in birds, did a backyard bird count, and wrote a persuasive essay for school on migratory birds. During spring break, we're in the back yard, and we look up and see a male cardinal singing in the tree. Neither one of us had realized that cardinals had a song. Helen listens, looks at the bird, and whistles its song back to it. The bird looks at her and whistles it back. The cardinal ended up coming up to the porch and they whistled back and forth. I don't know if the bird thought she was a female cardinal or what!

"We have also had a peregrine falcon in our yard. There's one at the Shrine [at nearby Catholic University]—so when Helen saw it she knew what it was right away. She was just beside herself! She called this friend of ours in New Jersey who's really interested in birds; he's like fifty years old compared to Helen's eleven! Helen left a message: 'I'm sorry you're not home! THERE'S A PERE-GRINE FALCON IN OUR YARD!'

"The more Helen learns about birds, the more things open up to her, and the more things she discovers about them. She has questions, she explores, she notices. To me, that's education, not the accumulation of little factoids that can be tested in school."

selves inspired to leave the conventional path and invent their own family's unique version of Guerrilla Learning.

Guerrilla Learning families:

- Take a creative approach to life and education
- Think and talk about what education is
- Think and talk about what they view as a successful life
- Value learning, involve their children in learning as a regular,

Both teachers, John and Randi Lewis send their son and daughter to a public elementary school. "We're not homeschoolers," says Randi, "partly because we're not in a position to homeschool—we like to eat regularly, for one thing!—but we're not traditional schoolers, either. To us, being awake is an opportunity to learn. We try to take the opportunity in whatever we're doing to learn. Everything is about education.

"For instance, we ride bikes together as a family. We stop whenever we see an opportunity to explore something, to find out about the world. My son is obsessed with insects. When he sees something he's interested in, we stop and study it. When we get home, we look it up in the encyclopedia. If there's not enough information there, we go to the library. Vacation is not necessarily just a vacation to us, because it's also an opportunity to learn new things.

"I love my children to be challenged and I want them more than anything to continue to love learning. But I'm not looking for them to learn skills any earlier than they are ready for. There are ways of being challenged and continuing to grow without being developmentally inappropriate! Education is not a race."

ongoing part of life, and continue to participate in the world of learning as adults

- Are sensitive to their children's evolving needs and abilities, knowing that what works may vary from child to child and that what works for one child may vary from year to year
- Advocate for their children at school
- Consider school to be one resource among many for their children's introduction into the "great conversations" of literature, science, the arts, and political life
- Give their children freedom to discover their own passions and talents and support them in pursuing those passions, even when they are not identical with government-defined school goals
- Participate in their communities, sharing their passion for learning with those who have fewer resources
- Know that to a great degree, children get their commitment to learning from their families and bring it to school—they don't get it from school

GETTING STARTED AT GUERRILLA LEARNING

I try never to let my schooling get in the way of my education.
—Mark Twain

The Gushues, the Lewises, and the other families whose stories we share in this book often differ markedly from one another in way of life, values, and parenting style. Yet they all have in common certain overall strategies in their approaches to education. The rest of this chapter discusses some of these strategies and how you can begin to explore them with your family. These strategies are:

- Create a larger context for thinking about your children's learning—a context larger than school.
- Reclaim the world of learning for your family.
- Become familiar with your kids' lives and schools.
- Lighten up about grades.
- Change the situation.

- Consider your children to be "creators-in-training."
- Unlock doors (and minds and hearts) with the "Five Keys" of true learning.

Create a Larger Context for Thinking about Your Children's Learning—A Context Larger Than School

One way of looking at schooling is that it's fancy job training. Kids need to learn how to read, write, and cipher—or the myriad modern equivalents thereof—so that they can go to high school, so that they can get into college, so that they can get good jobs. If your only model of a successful life is a person who performs outstandingly in school, is accepted to an exclusive college, again excels, is recruited for one of the top firms in the country at a high salary, and begins a life of corporate bliss, you should ignore this book and read one of the far more common books that help you figure out how to get your kids to do what you want them to do.

Then again, in our developing postindustrial, entrepreneurial society, Guerrilla Learners just might outperform those conventional winners in the long run. In fact, a recent study exploded the time-honored myth that going to an Ivy League school instead of an ordinary college gets you more money and a better job in the end. The authors concluded, in part, that "[s]tudents who attend elite colleges would probably end up with greater earnings capacity regardless of where they attend school," because successful applicants tend to have more discipline, ambition, imagination, maturity, and other characteristics that are rewarded with financial success. In other words, *students* create their success and make the schools look good. Students with similar characteristics who went to ordinary colleges do just as well in life, probably because at most colleges, students can get a good education if they try. "Companies prefer the competent from Podunk to the incompetent from Princeton," writes Robert Samuelson in the *Washington Post*, reporting on the study.[1]

---

[1] Robert Samuelson, "Overrating the Ivy League," *Washington Post*, October 27, 1999, p. A31. The study was by Alan Krueger, an economist at Princeton, and Stacy Berg Dale, a researcher at the Andrew W. Mellon Foundation.

We repeat: *Students create their success.* Learning may take place in schools, but learning is bigger than schools, and schools don't make learning; *learners* do. And you'll do your family a favor if you can turn conventional thinking on its head. Instead of seeing their learning only within the context of school, begin to see school as just one (of several) elements within the larger context of their learning. (By the same token, view academic learning in the context of your children's overall growth and character. Academics are not all-important; education should serve life, not the other way around.) When you really begin to see school as smaller than your kids' educations, you may find that you're able to relax and stop worrying as much about the markers of conventional success (or failure).

Many people imagine that some consensus exists among experts regarding what education is, what it's for, and what should be taught in American schools. There is, in fact, no such consensus. There are ongoing battles among policymakers, researchers, politicians, and groups such as teachers' unions about what should be taught, how it should be taught, who should decide the content and method, and what the purpose of all this activity is. Luckily, as Guerrilla Learners, we don't have to figure out what education is for everybody. We just have to figure out what it is for *us.* In some ways, the life of the mind is like the life of the spirit—it's private. That doesn't mean that we only want to learn in private, any more than freedom of religion means we only want to worship in private. (On the contrary, learning and worship—like dancing—often are greatly enhanced by being shared.) It does mean that critical choices about education (or religion) should be made by individuals, by families, and in neighborhoods, not by government bureaucracies.

Our working definition of education? Real education allows us to participate in the great conversation that is literature, science, the

Susan Gushue: "We talk with our children about what a successful life is. Actually, it's more like we try to *show* them. To us, being able to pursue the things you're interested in is a successful life. Our children can see this not only by looking at our lives but by looking at our friends' lives. We tend to spend time with people who have jobs that allow them to pursue what they're interested in. At the worst, they choose jobs that impede them the least.

"The thing at stake in all this is freedom. By letting your kids make choices, you let them see how free they really are. By choosing, they're constantly reminded that they're responsible. They will be less likely to confuse being coerced—by wanting to be part of a group—with not having a choice. You're teaching them something really important, which is: how to be free."

arts, history, and public life. An educated person is one who loves learning and is capable of continuing to partake of the shared human creative endeavor without being *forced*. Yes, such a person must acquire certain facts and skills to have that capacity. But it's the depth and authenticity of his or her connection to that knowledge, and not its breadth or "testability," that matters.

That's our vision (for now—it changes from time to time). Your definition might be vastly different. *The power of creating a larger context for your children's education is in developing a vision that inspires you as individuals and as a family.* You might even develop a vision of education among your group of friends, or in your neighborhood, that the kids help work out and share. Make no mistake: Questioning school's

Thomas and Lisa Dunn of Massapequa Park, New York, have four children, ages one to eight. Their children attend the local public elementary school, which the Dunns feel is very family-oriented and encourages parental involvement.

"My husband and I feel that we are the primary educators of our children and accept responsibility for it," says Lisa. "We do not just talk about education; we live the conversation. We are always seeking opportunities in life to learn for ourselves and to educate our children. We feel that in order to teach, we ourselves must be learners as well. I myself go to college on and off. My children especially love when I am in school. They love to ask me what I am learning and what my teacher is like.

"I have embraced the idea that it may take a village to raise a child but we as parents are ultimately responsible for learning and creating opportunities for our children. I look at my children's teachers as peers since we are all educators."

authority can be hard on kids. You will want your children to be very clear about the choices you are giving them the freedom to make and why your family is choosing to be "different." If your kids don't have a positive vision of their education for themselves, you run the risk that they will just feel weird and unsupported. You might choose to do what Amy does: She runs interference for her kids until they get to be twelve or so and then she begins to let them negotiate with teachers and school authorities on their own, unless they request support.

Reclaim the World of Learning for Your Family

Here is the most powerful way to cause a paradigm shift in the way you and your kids view education: *Start to see learning not as the province of experts but as the province of the family.* Learning belongs to *you*, not to schools and government administrators. It's a function of human wonder and curiosity and love for the world, and work skills are a small subset of that wonder. Children are born with an insatiable desire to learn. If your family is in love with learning, the rest will follow naturally. (Conversely, if your family is not in love with learning, your children will have to struggle to retain their sense of joy and wonder in learning.) This doesn't mean you have to be "well educated" in the competitive sense of the term. It just means that your family's relationship to the world of learning is a personal, private, and passionate one.

Omar and Aqiylah Collins, of Portland, Oregon, have three children who have variously attended public schools, attended private schools, and been homeschooled. Omar and Aqiylah first removed their eldest son and daughter, Fahiym and Hafidha, from New York City public schools when their daughter refused to submit herself to a strip search—an indignity that violated the family's Muslim beliefs. (The search was being routinely administered to all the children. When Hafidha refused, other girls began refusing as well.) The principal called Omar to request that he instruct Hafidha to submit to the search. Instead, her father removed her from school. The three children were then homeschooled for a number of years. Omar and Aquiyla's youngest son, Hanif, now attends a private Catholic school in the Portland area. Hafidha has graduated college and is working now, and Fahiym goes to Morehouse College.

"Just be involved at school, *be there*, let them see your face at least twice a week. You may not be aware of what goes on in there. . . . You have to be calling teachers on the phone, they have to be aware that you're a concerned parent. Parents think it's still like it once was, when you could just send your children to school and forget about them. If that day even existed, it's over now," advises Omar, a computer technician.

One of the cultural myths about school is that kids who aren't high achievers in school—who don't take the competition seriously enough—won't make it in life. They'll drop out, take drugs, get pregnant, end up working in fast food. The fallacy in this logic is that causes are confused with results. Low school achievement may be correlated with those outcomes because many kids who are poor school achievers also come from families where education is not valued or resources are not accessible. The hidden reality is that there are many families, with varying degrees of affluence and school achievement, in which education is highly valued but school is taken with a grain of salt.

Become Familiar with Your Kids' Lives and Schools

If your time allows, get involved in your child's school as a volunteer. The relationships you form and the insights you gain into what goes on inside school walls will be invaluable. If time won't permit you to commit to a certain number of hours, see if you can arrange to visit. If your kids are embarrassed to have you in their classrooms, you could attend on a day without them, or—if they attend a middle school or high school—go to a different section of the same class.

Susan Gushue advises, "You can make a community for your children at their school by talking to their teachers, the security guard, the cafeteria lady, and taking the time to get to know people. That way, when things aren't working for your child, you already have a relationship with the people you need to ask for help. It also means you'll get information from the adults before it gets too bad. People will feel more comfortable calling you or talking to you when you drop your child off. Their only interaction with you isn't when there's a problem."

Similarly, get involved in your kids' homework—not just to help

A music producer and a business consultant, Steve Phillips and Becky Pryor of St. Louis, Missouri, homeschooled their three children until their oldest was ten. Then they made the decision, for economic and other reasons, to send them to school. Now, according to Becky, "We make it a priority to have dinner together as a family and talk about what's going on. We discuss how the children see things, what's going on at school, how they're feeling about it, and how it fits into our family's values.

"We encourage our kids to study and do well, but we emphasize that grades and test scores are just one measure of how they're doing at any one point in time. It's just one piece in the big puzzle. We remind our kids that standardized testing reflects less about who they are, individually, than about how the educational system operates. We often work with the school advocating for a more authentic education for our children.

"There was a situation in our daughter's fourth-grade science class that was very uncomfortable for her. It was a rat experiment which was sponsored by the dairy council (my mom used to teach it to her students in the 1960s–1970s). One rat was fed a 'healthy' diet, including a lot of dairy products (which rats don't eat); the other rat was basically starved by being fed a junk-food diet. The rats were weighed and measured and graphed to show that the one on the dairy [healthier] diet was growing faster. After a couple of weeks, dairy was introduced into the stunted rat's diet to show how its growth spiked upward. We looked at some of the handouts, and the handouts were full of propaganda.

"Our main priority was to speak up for our daughter. She was not comfortable with the animals' suffering: the incarceration, feeding them an unnatural diet, and purposely starving the rat. We wanted to be certain that she would have an acceptable alternative to the experiment. Second, it was a unit on nutrition. As parents wanting to guide our child to make the healthiest food choices, we had a problem with the dairy council's definition of 'healthy choice.' We have dairy allergies in our family and don't consume dairy at all at our house. We are able to get plenty of calcium and to grow strong, healthy bones and bodies from a diet rich in botanical nutrients, but those options were only vaguely mentioned in the curriculum!

"Becky happened to be on campus the day the dairy council representative made her final presentation. The dairy rep displayed X rays of two rats (not of the actual rats used in the experiment) to show how the rat which was fed the diet rich in dairy had greater bone density. She played some naming games with the kids which were meant to promote a healthy diet. For all proposed questions, a dairy choice was always the 'best' answer. "What is an infant's first food?" she asked the class. The answer—[cow's] milk! She said that they would have the opportunity for Q&As, but there was no opportunity given. It seemed to us like the experiment was more for entertainment than real science.

"We wrote a letter to the school suggesting that students need to have alternative choices to animal experiments. We also expressed our strong opinion that commercial interests have no place in schools."

them, and certainly not to do it for them or even to make them do it—but to see what they're really working on and what you think of it. You may be amused by what's in some textbooks, from your adult viewpoint, if you haven't looked lately.

Lighten Up about Grades

There are *many* paths to a successful adult life. Don't pretend there's only one. The United States isn't Japan, where success in nursery school can (supposedly) determine a child's future employment prospects. The United States is an embarrassment of riches where entrepreneurship rules, and any adult with energy and creativity and persistence and a little native intelligence can figure out a way to make a livelihood. Furthermore, the U.S. economy is moving further and further away from the industrial model, where conformity, obedience, and dependence on one institution were rewarded. The skills and information that kids get in school can be useful, of course, and academic success can lead to success in one kind of adult existence— being in a profession that requires those credentials. Unfortunately, the exhausting obstacle course of school often extinguishes the very creativity, persistence, and focus that adults in other kinds of work need. Ask your friends how they got qualified for what they do and what school had to do with it. Break the cultural trance of pretense about school experience, and you might begin to connect with your children—who may not have started pretending yet, since they are the ones currently suffering—in a new way. *Show children many models of success.* Don't automatically disparage people who don't finish college (or even high school), or who pursue trades, or who don't make a lot of money. Our culture markets the myth that academic success is the one true path to happiness, security, and success in life.

"My wife and I believe that children are natural learners," says Michael Soguero, a senior high school science and math teacher at a New York City public high school and the father of four young boys. "It's more important to tap into and support a child's natural curiosity than it is to ensure things like grade-level expectations and the like. . . . Families are instrumental in helping to support this natural curiosity."

If your family will need tuition assistance for college, which is often tied to high school grades, make that goal, and the precise reasons for it, clear to your children. Instead of implying "You have to get good grades or you'll be a failure," you can tell them, "Let's figure out a way for you to get a B average so that we can get financial aid." As early as

---

Becky Pryor: "Our three children were attending a very good school, and the two older kids were very happy there. Our youngest son, Elliott, however, resisted going to kindergarten about halfway through the year. He was interested in learning. The problem for him was that he would get engaged with what he was doing, and having to shift gears and do something else was difficult for him. He also felt that what he had to say didn't matter at school—he felt like he didn't have a voice. I really liked his two kindergarten teachers. I felt like I related to them on a soul level. So we persevered and made it through that year.

"In first grade, however, his assigned teacher had to leave and was replaced by a teacher with twenty-five years of experience teaching *sixth* graders. Her whole class was about control and conformity. She had a rewards system on the bulletin board. If the students were good, they got a piece of paper popcorn. The kids who accumulated full bags of popcorn were promised a popcorn party. 'I guess I wasn't good today,' Elliott remarked when he got home. I talked to the principal, who is against that kind of thing, and the system was discontinued the next day.

"Elliott got put in a corner the first day of school—he didn't hear the teacher say that the class was not allowed to talk. I couldn't imagine him doing it to be disruptive. I spoke to his teacher and her response was 'Well, I told the class several times, and we had to remove him.' Elliott's concern was not that he had been made an example of in front of the class. He complained that he was cold—he was put by the air conditioner—and he said that he never heard the teacher say that he couldn't talk. Besides, he was drawing, and he thought that the class should be able to converse.

"Elliott's sensory perception seemed to reflect a bigger concern of mine: that warmth and flexibility were lacking in his classroom. I observed the class on other mornings, and all I can say is that I had this realization that Elliott would adapt, he would adapt fine. But at what point does one's spirit start getting crushed? I wanted the teacher to see our son as an individual and to help him unfold.

"We had difficult financial constraints. But my kid was not happy. I saw his institutionalized school experience as something that was dampening his spirit. I said yes, I can do this, I can homeschool my child—he needs it. There's a great secular homeschooling support group in Kansas City called L.E.A.R.N. (Let Education Always Remain Natural) that I joined. I'm still adjusting, trying to figure out how to make time for myself. I've got Elliott during the day as well as my other children at night—I want to be available for each of them and their activities. It's definitely challenging, trying to find time for my own interests and to feed my own soul. You just do what you have to do, and somehow it just works. Part of it's about compromise; part of it's about sacrifice; all of it's about investment. In the long run I can't see us regretting any time that we've made to be with our kids. It boils down to you having to look into your own heart and doing what you feel is right for your kid. Nobody else can tell you what that is."

possible, help teenagers decide exactly where they want to go to college and exactly what requirements must be met. Doing so can help replace panic and confusion about imaginary standards with solid, reality-based goals.

Stephanie Hunter, of Culpeper, Virginia, is the single mother of a now nine-year-old boy named Stephen. Stephanie has taught kindergarten for five years in a public school, where Stephen also attended school for his kindergarten through second-grade years. This is her story of their journey through those years.

"When I think back on that time, I am still filled with a certain anguish for my son," writes Stephanie. "I know that I always did the best I could for him with the understanding I possessed at the time, and as my understanding grew, along with it came the absolute certainty that Stephen's happiness, peace of mind, and confidence in his own beautiful and unique abilities mattered more to me than anything else, certainly more than his so-called lack of progress within the public school system. But there were many hard days to come before I knew in my gut that the wrongness of what was happening to him as the special individual he is within that system was something I had the power to do something about.

"First of all, Stephen didn't enjoy kindergarten, his first year of school, as much as I had hoped he would, especially toward the end as the pressure mounted regarding beginning reading skills and readiness for first grade. The curriculum included, at that point, writing in the computer lab every day and even some standardized testing to assess early reading skills, as well as a home reading program. At the end of the year, his teacher gently suggested a lack of maturity and recommended that he be in a special program in the first grade. In Culpeper, this program is presently called the Multi-Year Program, and it is used to bolster the academic abilities of children considered at risk for not being able to attain, or maintain, predetermined grade-level reading skills in an average first-grade classroom. Class size is limited, two teachers are present, summer school is available and highly suggested, and the children stay with the same teachers through the second-grade year as well—hence the title.

"In Stephen's case, in a nutshell, the program simply didn't work according to theory. By the middle of his first-grade year his teacher had suggested I take him to his pediatrician for an evaluation for possible attention deficit disorder (ADD). Not knowing any better and not understanding yet that the apparent deficit was in large part defined by its context and not necessarily present in the child, and in spite of my misgivings, I followed through on her suggestion. I longed for my son to feel positive about himself as a learner, and I accepted the opinions of those with many more years of experience than I, in the hope that an answer lay ahead. Stephen was diagnosed with ADD and Ritalin was prescribed.

"How does one explain to a young (seven-year-old) boy, already convinced that he lacked in intelligence, why this medicine is necessary without making him feel even less successful? I ached for Stephen. Homework times were no less stressful, and in fact the effect of 'coming down' off the Ritalin was nothing short of horrifying for both of us. After two weeks of startling late-afternoon episodes of what I'd have to call total blow-ups/breakdowns on Stephen's part, all triggered by the frustration of having an overload of homework, I notified the pediatrician that we were through with Ritalin, no matter what. Citing possible dips in serotonin levels in the brain and other medical jargon that I didn't understand, she suggested and then prescribed a new medication, Adderall.

"While his teacher then reported that to her great relief Stephen was indeed more attentive, he was not happier about school or any more self-motivated than before. (He had never had a behavior problem, and he continued to be well liked by his peers during this time.) Homework time continued to be stressful for Stephen.

"Over the summer between his first- and second-grade years, Stephen was able to stop his medication, but as soon as school started he began taking it again. However, during Christmas vacation I consistently observed what appeared to be the symptoms of depression occurring late morning—not long before his second dose. When I reported this to his doctor, she prescribed a second medication, Wellbutrin, an antidepressant, to alleviate the effects of the first. Mind you, short of an occasional aspirin, I rarely take any sort of medication myself, so you can imagine the bells going off in my head over all the medication my son was on. However, I felt some relief for him when his mood equilibrium seemed largely restored as a result of taking this new medication.

"In the spring of his second-grade year, Stephen was tested for a learning disability within the school system. The tests were inconclusive. Still stuck in the assumption that someone smarter than me must be able to ascertain why Stephen was having problems learning to read, I eventually took him to the Kluge Children's Rehabilitation Center at the University of Virginia (where diagnostic testing for learning disabilities is available) for a long day of rigorous testing. There were still no conclusive results.

"I began to listen more closely to an inner voice, and a shift took place inside me. I let go of my blind acceptance of what the experts all around were saying to me. I began to look for alternatives for Stephen's education, based on a growing conviction that the problem had never been my son's, although, as a teacher, I'd been subliminally taught that it certainly couldn't be the school system's either. Then a friend told me about a parent-governed cooperative school that could offer us a partial scholarship. I paid them a few visits to talk with teachers and parents and to observe the students in action. Finally, one day I took Stephen out of school early, and he and I met with the woman who would be his teacher, if we chose to go there. She spent some time with him, working and drawing, and chatting, very informally. Very quietly and simply, after a moment of thought she said, 'I think he just needs some *time*.' I sat and thought—time to grow, time to play, time to be a child and to learn as children will learn. And I simply wept. It was the first time a teacher had spoken about Stephen with compassion for him as a child first and foremost, not with cold test results and clinical comments on his *failure* to meet standardized expectations. This teacher, who only recently had met Stephen, understood intuitively and trusted that he would develop as he was ready, and she honored that. It confirmed my deepest sense of my son as a sensitive, bright, loving, and vivacious person.

"Today Stephen is off all medications and attends the school we visited. He is still reluctant to read, although the basic ability to do so is in him. Part of that is simply who he is, and part of that may also be the lingering effect of having it indirectly suggested to him for so long that he wasn't up to par, that he was behind, that he scored low and fell short. He knew how his teachers perceived him, and he suffered for it.

"It wasn't a matter of courage, taking Stephen out of that situation. It was a matter of learning to stop all the outside voices, including the voice of my own fear, and truly listen to my son. It was a matter of discarding pat answers and simply doing what was best for the most important person in my life. If I could say anything to parents in similar straits, I would say this: Listen to your heart about what is best for your children, even when the loudest voices around you are not in harmony with yours. *Follow your heart, always.* You are the best and most important advocate your child has, and no teacher, no doctor, no system, no expert anywhere understands your child like you do. Trust that. I did, and our lives were changed."

﹐ation

﹐st of this book focuses on new ways of thinking that can
﹐ur day-to-day interactions with our kids, there's no denying
﹐ some large-scale changes might also benefit some families. These
changes include homeschooling, alternative schools, charter schools,
and activism. We'll discuss them briefly here and give you more
information in Appendix B, "Alternatives to Traditional Schooling."

Homeschooling

Consider homeschooling for all or part of your child's education. If
you can and are willing to, homeschooling is a fantastic option. But
it's not all or nothing. It's certainly not for all families, or for all children; homeschooling may even work for a particular child one year
and not the next. Even if you don't think you could ever be a "career"
homeschooler—one who takes kids out of school once and for all—
there are many creative ways to experiment temporarily, incremen-
tally, or imaginatively with homeschooling.

For example, the Gushues send their kids to public schools where
there are schools that serve the kids' needs but aren't afraid to take
them out when their children need something different. For
instance, Charles spent sixth through eighth grades at home—"reading and going to museums," according to Susan—and then returned
to the public school that has an emphasis on the fine and perform-
ing arts for ninth grade. One eighth-grade teacher remarked to
Susan that keeping kids home in seventh and eighth grade isn't such
a bad idea for any family! Other families have kept kids home during
one or two particularly difficult years, when kids were being teased or
bullied, struggling with emotional problems, or simply seemed to
need some quality time with their families. These kids returned to
school more confident, more connected to their parents, more sure
of their goals—and sometimes more appreciative of what school has
to offer. (See Appendix B for homeschooling resources.)

Alternative Schools

Or consider enrolling your kids in a different school. Explore schools
that use Montessori, Waldorf, and other time-tested methods that
respect children's developmental timetables, honor the intercon-

nectedness of all knowledge, and understand the power of experiential learning. In Appendix B, we include brief descriptions of some of our favorite types of alternative schooling as well as resources to help you find out more about them. These alternatives are mostly private or cooperative schools, although some (such as Montessori) exist in the public school system, and all can be potentially adopted by charter schools, depending on the state. If you really wish to send your child to an alternative school, depending on where you live, you probably can find one that will work for you and with you, even if you have financial limitations.

Charter Schools

In an increasing number of states, charter school legislation makes it possible for groups of parents, educators, and community members to found their own publicly funded school. The school must be nonsectarian, nonexclusive, and meet other criteria, but once approved, these schools can operate with a large degree of autonomy compared to ordinary public schools. Governing legislation varies from state to state. Charter schools are an exciting, promising alternative for energetic, committed community groups and parents to design and run schools according to their unique shared vision. In some states, alternatives such as Waldorf or Montessori schools have been established and publicly funded through charter legislation.

Activism

Perhaps you're an activist, and you have a vision for the school your kids now attend and want to commit time and energy toward working to improve that school. You don't want to be an escapist or make things better for your own kids by simply abandoning your neighborhood school. If that's your choice, then more power to you. Your efforts may indeed result in a better situation, if not for your kids then for others down the line. Or if they don't seem to have any effect, at least they might help raise public awareness.

Just don't set yourself up for disappointment. Be sure any efforts you undertake seem worth it to you, even if you don't manage to make big changes. One way to do this would be to make a personal study of the best school reform literature—read John Holt, Maria

Montessori, Ivan Illich, Howard Gardner, and then at least you and your children are sure to benefit from your broader perspective. (See "Chapter Two Resources" for information on books by these writers.) Or make a personal project out of becoming a powerful activist, or a fearless public speaker, or whatever. Keep in mind that many dedicated people have given their lives over to school reform, for decades, with relatively little result. Also be aware that if you fight to bring progressive programs into your school, you may be opposed by well-organized parent groups who want tougher standards and more testing. Be gentle and patient with yourself, and focus on the things you can definitely change—such as the way you deal with your own kids' learning—at the same time that you fight the good fight.

Consider Your Children to Be "Creators-in-Training"

> "I have not failed. I have successfully discovered
> 1200 ideas that don't work."
> —*Thomas Edison*

The great biologist and psychologist Jean Piaget wrote, "The principal goal of education is to create men who are capable of doing new things, not simply of repeating what other generations have done— men who are creative, inventive and discoverers."[2]

What do creators look like? Where do they come from? Certainly they do not always show promise in conventional schools—indeed, many of them never attended conventional schools. The following portraits illustrate what we mean by "creators."

- *Richard Feynman*, who was a brilliant student (his high school geometry teacher, Mr. Augsbury, said, "I give up," and invited Richard to teach the class), credited his father with encouraging his love of inquiry. Feynman won the Nobel Prize for physics in 1965. Feynman's insatiable curiosity and passion for life led him to become an artist, a drummer, a safe-cracker, and a world-class

---

[2] Jean Piaget, *The Moral Judgement of the Child* (London: Routledge, 1932).

practical joker. (While a young physicist at the top-secret Manhattan Project during the development of the atomic bomb, Feynman delighted in surreptitiously breaking into the secure files of the other physicists and leaving flippant notes.) Serving on the committee investigating the cause of the 1986 *Challenger* space shuttle disaster, Feynman famously demonstrated the problem by dunking a sample of the henceforth-notorious "O-ring" material into his glass of ice water.

- *Margaret Mead* was educated by her missionary parents. Her mother took advantage of their frequent posting changes by having the children tutored by local artisans in skills such as basketry and weaving. Although currently under fire, Mead's renowned studies of child rearing, personality, and culture permanently altered the way people—from trained anthropologists to ordinary folk—understand marriage and family life.

- *Gordon Parks* bluffed his way into a job as a photographer when he was a poor, teenage runaway in the 1920s. In addition to working as a *LIFE* magazine photojournalist for twenty-four years, Parks became the first black director of a full-length film (*The Learning Tree*, from the novel he wrote); directed the first film featuring a black romantic hero (*Shaft*); wrote fiction, nonfiction, and poetry, painted and composed, wrote the music and libretto for a ballet (*Martin*); and received over fifty honorary degrees and awards although he never graduated from high school.

- *Laurens van der Post*, a writer who grew up in the African bush without formal schooling, brought the plight of the Bushmen to the attention of his friend Carl Jung and later the world. As a young officer in a World War II Japanese concentration camp, van der Post created a school for the other inmates to help pass the time and keep morale high. Fifteen men received diplomas, written on the concentration camp's toilet paper, which were later recognized by "official" universities.

Why do we mention these creative geniuses? Certainly not to imply that your child, properly educated, must become a glorious overachiever. Rather, we want to illustrate our contention that real education is fundamentally about independent thinking and creativity,

Chapter Two: What We Can Do

✐

EXERCISES

For you: Spend some time thinking about what education is and what you see as its purpose. Talk about it to your spouse or other adults in your family. Write it down, revise it, discuss it with friends and other parents. Do more reading about education if you like. (See Chapter 1's Resources for some starting ideas.) This is the ongoing inquiry that will reclaim learning for your family.

For your kids: At the same time, discuss the following ideas with your kids. Ask them what their definition of education would be. Talk to them about what you view as a successful life, and ask them for their views. See if you can agree on a simple statement expressing your family's view of the purpose of education. Write it down—and illustrate it, if there are visual artists among you—and stick it on the fridge. Invite family members to change or improve it as time goes by.

not about vocational training or competition. What interests us most about Feynman, Mead, Parks, and van der Post is not how brilliant or celebrated they were but how fascinated they were with all of life, with exploring many different unrelated areas, with seeing things in new and unpredictable ways, and, above all, with bringing into being what hadn't been there before.

The phrase "creative person" is redundant: *Every* child is born creative. True education includes gaining familiarity with the products and processes—the stories—of powerfully creative people of the past *so that we can join in the game.* Our culture overly concerns itself with "creativity," or the ability to imagine unusual stuff, and demonstrates insufficient concern with "creating," or the ability to turn what you imagine into something that can be shared with others.

Unfortunately, most schools systematically eradicate the very skills that creators need. They reward success and punish failure, stifling experimentation and creativity. They teach children to perform meaningless tasks to please arbitrary authorities at the expense of their own thoughts, feelings, and purposes. You succeed at what you're told to do in school, or you're regarded as a failure. Any project or purpose you may dream up on your own is irrelevant.

Robert Fritz, in his book *Creating*, identifies the problem: "There are two kinds of people . . . those who see life as a performance and those who see life as a work in progress. Performers and learners. The strange irony is that our educational system is designed to produce performers, not learners. The emphasis is on successful performance rather than on successful learning. There are penalties for failure and rewards for accomplishment, *as if failure and learning were separate*" (our italics).[3]

In order to learn to be a creator, you have to be encouraged to listen to your inner voice. You have to take a lot of time trying and failing at many different projects of your own design. You must be willing, like Thomas Edison, to fail most of the time. (Edison's mother, by the way, angrily withdrew him from school to teach him at home because at school he was considered abnormal and mentally ill.) It probably helps to be encouraged to care more about what you think of yourself and your work than what others think. Creators must learn to emphasize process rather than product.

Of course, many children preserve their delight and fascination with creating; many even thrive as creators in the school environment. But many others get the message too loud, too deep in their bones: *Just do what you're told. What you want doesn't matter.* Finally, too much of school's method is downright antithetical to what is required in learning to be a creator. One of the opportunities for Guerrilla Learning families is the opportunity to encourage children's dreams and projects, even those that don't explicitly relate to school goals, precisely to allow them practice in the essential skill-set that creators need.

Creating need not be flashy or dramatic. It can be simple and subtle: sharing your writing with a few friends who can appreciate it. Designing and building birdhouses. Building a Web site for your local nonprofit group. Sewing your own curtains using fabric found in a

---

[3] Robert Fritz, *Creating* (New York: Fawcett Books, 1991), p. 79.

thrift shop. Baking a really fine pie. Organizing a neighborhood cleanup. Writing about your family's experience caring for a relative with Alzheimer's disease, and seeing your writing published in your church newsletter. Any time we bring persistence and imagination to bear on a vision, whether individual or shared, we are creating.

Unlock Doors (and Minds and Hearts) with the "Five Keys" of True Learning

Understanding and honoring five fundamental principles can transform the way you relate to your kids and greatly assist them in growing up to be joyful, passionate creators. What's more, you might just transform the way you look at the world, opening up new possibilities for yourself. Some or all of these fundamental principles are most likely familiar to you. But we feel they're so essential—and so little understood—that we need to devote a chapter to each of them. And we will in the pages that follow.

Focus on the Five Keys, and many of the other things we mention in this chapter will fall into place. You'll find that you're nourishing creativity, relaxing about grades, treating school as one element within the larger context of your family's educational enterprise, and viewing your children—and maybe yourself—in a new way. In the next chapter, with help from our Guerrilla Learning families, we begin to describe the Five Keys.

Resources

Armstrong, Thomas, Ph.D. *The Myth of the ADD Child: 50 Ways to Improve Your Child's Behavior and Attention Span without Drugs, Labels, or Coercion.* Plume, 1997.

Fritz, Robert. *Creating.* New York: Fawcett Books, 1993.

Gardner, Howard. *Frames of Mind: The Theory of Multiple Intelligences.* New York: Basic Books, 1993

Gleick, James. *Genius: The Life and Science of Richard Feynman.* New York: Pantheon, 1992.

Hasten Slowly: The Journey of Sir Laurens van der Post. A film by Mickey Lemle. Lemle Pictures, Inc., 1996.

Holt, John. *How Children Learn.* Cambridge: Perseus Press, 1995.

Hutchings, Edward, (ed.). *Surely You're Joking, Mr. Feynman: Adventures of a Curious Character.* New York: W. W. Norton & Company, 1985, 1997.

Illich, Ivan, et al. *Deschooling Society.* New York: Marion Boyers, Inc., 1999

Mead, Margaret. *Blackberry Winter: My Earlier Years.* Tokyo: Kodansha International, 1972, 1995.

Montessori, Maria. *Discovery of the Child.* New York: Ballantine, 1996.

Parks, Gordon. *Voices in the Mirror: An Autobiography.* New York: Doubleday, 1990.

3

The Five Keys to Guerrilla Learning

Amy: My daughter Carsie could read at the age of three. Stringing together sounds and thus deciphering words was a pleasant, exciting game for her, which we played using paper and pencil or our voices alone.

Yet my son, Elijah, had an entirely different experience. Like many American children, he was exposed at an early age to what experts call "reading readiness" skills—the shape and sound of letters, the idea of direction, words' initial sounds—through preschool, TV, books, games, and interaction with family and friends. By the age of four, Elijah could identify each letter and the sound it made. However, when asked to consider a string of letters and put the sounds together, he was lost. He would guess wildly, or guess random words with the same initial sound ("BEAR? BABY? BOAT?!!!").

As Elijah turned five, and then six, he became more interested in learning to read. He would ask, "What does that sign say?" He'd painstakingly write notes to people, asking those around him how to spell each word letter by letter. He would study the cover of a favorite book and ask, "Which word is 'disaster'?" He would scan a page of a Godzilla adventure book and find all the *z*s. Or he would see *z*s in tree branches, in the clouds, in the green beans on his plate. (Interestingly, this obsession with *z*s coincided with his absorption in the movie *Zorro*.) However, if I showed him a word and asked him to try to read it, usually in the context of a game, he would freeze more often than not, his anxiety and confusion displacing his grasp of all the necessary elements. Each time this happened, I backed off, waiting weeks or months before gently reintroducing an opportunity.

One night, when Elijah was six and a half, we sat down with a stack of bedtime stories and opened the first book, an "easy reader" about barnyard animals. Elijah's eye fell on the first page and he immediately poked a finger at the print. "That says 'dog,'" he declared. "Yes, it does," I affirmed. He dropped his jaw and looked at me with an expression hovering between glee and bewilderment. He looked back at the book. "What is this word?" I asked. He looked where I was pointing, soundlessly moving his lips. "PIG!" he cried. "YES!" I shouted. He turned back to me, now fully gleeful. "Show me another one!" he demanded. Over the next few minutes he read eight more words. He sounded out each word at first, then recognized it on sight when it appeared on another page. After years of preparation, he suddenly got it.

Later Elijah's dad entered the room and we shared Elijah's great breakthrough with him. He was appropriately impressed. After Elijah finished jumping up and down on the bed shouting "I can read! I can read!" he sat back down and I read him more stories. His eyelids drooped. My husband turned on the TV. Elijah opened one eye and glanced at the screen. "That says 'TV3,'" he announced sleepily. He was reading the station's ID logo in the corner of the screen.

We include this story to illustrate what we call the Five Keys to Guerrilla Learning. They are concepts that will help you understand how to make Guerrilla Learning a part of your child's, and your, world. As you begin to see your child's learning and development through these key concepts, your relationship with your child, and your attitude toward his or her learning, will shift profoundly.

What are the Five Keys? They are: *opportunity, timing, interest, freedom* and *support*.

OPPORTUNITY

In Elijah's story, *opportunity* is expressed in the way he was surrounded by books, reading, prereading materials and games, and a family culture that values literacy.

TIMING

We were sensitive to Elijah's innate *timing* by gently introducing reading occasions that would allow him (and us) to discover whether he was ready to put together his skills and understanding and make the leap to literacy.

Interest

We let Elijah's *interest* lead, waiting until he himself *wanted* to read for his own purposes rather than trying to "make" him read beyond his interest.

Freedom

We gave Elijah the *freedom* to choose when, where, and what he read and to generate his own timing and interest without imposing our own timetable or demands.

Grace: When I was four years old, my mother (who had noticed that I liked to dress up and leap around to music, though I'd never seen any dance performed) took me to a ballet recital. I vividly remember watching girls not much older than me swirl about on the stage, as well as the older teenagers, who glided and spun gracefully in ethereal, shining costumes. I was enthralled and delighted, unaware that the experience could get any better, until my mother turned to me and said, "Would you like to do that?" Even now I can recall the full, soaring feeling I got in my chest when she asked me that. Though I had blissfully watched the show, it hadn't occurred to me that there could be any connection between me and those sequined fairy princesses on the stage.

I soon started ballet lessons, which I kept up—usually enthusiastically—for the next nine years, and which segued into flings with jazz, tap, modern, African, drill team, and flamenco dance. Eventually I entered into longer romances with gymnastics and international folk dancing and ultimately into a beloved side career: I became a performer and teacher of my favorite dance form: Middle Eastern, or "belly dance."

SUPPORT

Finally, we were there with *support* when it was needed and wanted—giving Elijah materials, explaining, celebrating his breakthrough, and, perhaps most important, witnessing his success.

Guerrilla Learning revolves around these key concepts. Almost *all* learning is dependent on opportunity, timing, interest, freedom, and support—and we can observe these concepts at work, time and again, in our own lives and in the lives of our children.

Notice how in the example on page 63, all five qualities came together quickly in one moment and then continued throughout Grace's ballet career. Grace's mother noticed her *interest* in music and movement and, on a hunch, took her to a show—*opportunity*. The *timing* was right, and when her mother asked whether Grace wanted lessons (more *opportunity*, and the *freedom* for Grace to choose for herself), she immediately chose to pursue her *interest*. Her mother then provided *support* by checking out the two main ballet schools in town and enrolling her in the best one, driving her once or twice weekly to class for the next nine years, sewing dozens of costumes and fussing with her stage makeup, checking with doctors to make sure Grace wouldn't hurt her feet by wearing pointe shoes, and—along with Grace's father—attending her recitals, cheering her on, and paying for all those lessons.

It's easy for adults to take these fundamentals for granted, because as free agents we supply most of them for ourselves—or, if we don't, we fail to notice. We take it for granted that if we want to learn something, we can do so. Of course, we may have self-defeating thoughts—"When will I ever find the time to attend that poetry group?"—or we may inhibit ourselves with barely conscious beliefs—"I could never start running at my age"—but unless we have a particularly controlling spouse, we don't butt up against much serious resistance outside of ourselves. As adults in a wealthy society, we have the power to learn just about anything—to choose and then follow through on any project. Kids—particularly young kids, but teenagers too—aren't as powerful as we are. They need more support and nurturing to really pursue their passions, and they're probably not going to get enough of it from school.

So how do the Five Keys work together? Opportunity and support are gifts that you as a parent can actively provide. Freedom is more neutral—something we hope you'll *allow* your kids to have more of, even though you may have been strongly conditioned against that. And timing and interest are what your children bring to the table, something parents need to learn to accept and honor.

It's true that each of us naturally inclines more toward some keys than others. Some parents are generous in giving support but fearful about granting freedom. Others are relaxed and trusting, and easily allow their children the freedom to grow, but are preoccupied and protective of their own time; they are resistant to being asked for too much support.

Some parents, instead of respecting a child's greatest interests, reframe them as "hobbies" or "extracurriculars," thus basically dismissing them. Many times they twist one of the keys around and inadvertently wind up expressing its "shadow side." Instead of open-heartedly offering their children opportunities, these parents pressure their children into joining them in what motivates *them*.

One of the most important things parents can do is to become self-aware. We need to notice if we are afraid to give our children freedom, or if we feel guilty about opportunities we have not been able to provide for them. We can recognize that we feel reluctant to support them, that we judge and criticize their interests, or that we are anxious about the pace at which they learn and do things. Only by becoming aware of our *own* fears will we be able to transform ourselves to truly honor our children's relationship with the realm of learning.

To help you integrate these concepts into your thinking, we'll redefine and enlarge each key concept in the chapters that follow. We then offer exercises, at least one of which is geared toward *you*, so that you experience the benefits of each key from the inside out, and others you can undertake on behalf of your children, so that you can change the way you view their learning rather than simply try out a bunch of new strategies on them. Kids are often suspicious when their parents experiment with new techniques, particularly when they can't sense any clear intention or loving and logical foundation underneath those techniques. In fact, part of the benefit of doing the exercises we suggest *for you* is that it will help your kids feel that you're all in this together and thus will enable them to be more trusting of your efforts on their behalf.

The chapters themselves offer practical "strategies," too, because once you begin to make important shifts in your thinking and perception, your *actions* are next on the list of priorities. There are plenty of concrete things you can do to enhance your kids' learning. While the exercises will help you shift your perspective and understand your children better, the strategies are outward, sometimes more practical, intended for short-term or even immediate results.

Finally, each "key" chapter includes what we call "the heart of the key": a simple way to connect your behavior with your children's needs so you can remember easily what to do.

But enough preamble. There's no time like the present. We suggest you try an exercise (or three!) *now*.

Chapter Three: The Five Keys

EXERCISES

For you: Think of something you've chosen to learn as an adult. Identify how *opportunity, timing, interest, freedom,* and *support* contributed to your learning. Did a teacher, spouse, friend, or other adult make a significant contribution?

Remember something you learned as a child. Identify how *opportunity, timing, interest, freedom,* and *support* played into your learning. What did your parents contribute? How did they get in the way? Who else helped or hindered you? What would have helped you learn better?

Remember something you were asked to learn as a child, but didn't want to or couldn't. Which of the Five Keys were missing? What was the experience like for you?

Finally, think of something you were interested in or wanted to learn as a child but didn't learn or gave up on. What stopped you? Was there a lack of opportunity, freedom, or support? What did others say about you, and did you believe it? What did you decide about yourself?

For your children: Think of something one of your children has learned recently, and again, identify the interplay of the Five Keys. How did your attention to each of the Five Keys contribute to your child's learning experience? Was attention to any of the keys missing? Might it have made a difference if it were present?

Think of something one of your children wanted to learn and didn't. Again, focus on the Five Keys. Were one or more missing? What worked, and what didn't? What was that experience like for you?

Finally, think of something one of your children was assigned to learn by someone else but didn't want to learn. What was missing? What was the experience like for your child, according to your observation? What was the experience like for you?

4

Key #1

Opportunity

Education is about the only thing lying around loose in the world, and it's about the only thing a fellow can have as much of as he's willing to haul away.

—George Lorimer, *Letters of a Self-Made Merchant to His Son*

If the Five Keys to Guerrilla Learning are a building, opportunity is the ground floor, and it's furnished like a brightly lit, beckoning toy store. Opportunity is a new school year, a new millennium, a fresh start, a library packed with books you haven't read, the intriguing faces of strangers. To many of us, "opportunity" conjures images of barefoot immigrants transformed into busy butchers and bakers in this, the "land of opportunity." Opportunity is "golden." It sounds like an opening, not a commitment; possibilities, not requirements; new beginnings, not the drudgery of completion; surprises and serendipity, not routines; romance, not marriage; a smorgasbord, not leftovers. The truth is, of course, that commitment, completion, and routine are also essential and rewarding parts of life and learning. But they don't catch the imagination quite as much as our magic word: *opportunity*.

Of the Five Keys, opportunity is the most familiar in our school culture. Most experts, teachers, and parents understand that children need to be exposed often and early to a rich and varied environment in which books and reading are valued. Also widely accepted (although less often practiced) is the notion that the ideal educational climate involves *more* than books and reading. It includes exposure to a world of art and music, nature, science, meaningful conversation, philosophical and political questions, people from different cultures and walks of life, and attention to the life of the spirit. Like adults, children can figure out what they like, what they want, and what they're good at when they have plenty to choose from.

Many people think of "good schools" or elite colleges as the ultimate educational opportunities. Yet these institutions are not nearly as fundamental as a person's attitude, sense of personal power and possibility, and comfortable familiarity with a wide range of subjects and activities. If these qualities are well developed, many kids naturally experience schooling as stimulating and helpful. But in that case they also have what they will need to benefit from many other opportunities—a summer spent herding cattle, a visit to the Smithsonian Institution, a nature hike. And conversely, without this inner "preparedness," which is mostly provided by the family, kids will struggle to learn in any school they attend.

So read. Write. Talk. Play music together. Go see dance and theater and paintings. Read poetry, write poetry, get poetry refrigerator magnets. Spend time in nature. Build things. Go to museums—not as a school trip, but for love of the things you find there. Go to the library instead of the video store—it also offers great videos, but they're free and can be kept out longer in many areas. Most of these activities need not cost a dime. If you're not already doing these things, it's only because you've arranged your life so that you don't have time, and you've begun to believe that learning is something that happens not in life, but in school. The whole point of education is to be able to lead a rich and satisfying life, not to get a piece of paper that says you're entitled to a paycheck and a 401k plan. If you demonstrate that possibility with your life, not with your words, your children will hear you, loud and clear.

But don't do any of these things out of a sense of obligation or an ideal that you must offer enriching after-school activities to be a good parent. Do them only out of *love*. Read if you love reading. Talk if you love talking. Play the music you love. Do the things you love. Shakespeare is still read because he gives people joy, not because some expert decreed his work to be "great." Your kids will eventually find the joy in our cultural heritage if you do. It doesn't matter what aspect of it you participate in, as long as you do it with a grateful and eager heart. Make room for one thing you *love*—really focus on your own pleasure—and you'll soon want to make room for another, and you'll find a way to do so. If you raise your kids in such a home, you won't have to worry about their education. No one will be able to prevent them from being educated.

LIFE: IT'S AN OPEN-BOOK TEST

One more critical function of Guerrilla Learning is *answering children's questions*. Authentic learning grows out of wonder—out of the natural, spontaneous questioning that arises in children's attempts to understand their world and their position in it. Children are natural scientists, continuously making and improving a mental model of the world, testing hypotheses, integrating observations, and requesting information from adults to fill in the gaps or resolve inconsistencies. The beauty of answering children's questions spontaneously at home—Is there air on the moon? Where does wind come from? How fast does my heart beat? Can dogs and foxes have babies? How old do people live to be? What killed the dinosaurs?—is that the requested data is maximally meaningful at the moment the child requests it.

Not knowing the answers to kids' questions is not a problem but a wonderful, powerful opportunity to introduce them to the natural, satisfying process of *finding out* what we don't know. Amy finds she can answer most kids' questions until they reach the age of seven or so. After that, it's about 30 percent "here is the answer," 30 percent "I think it's like this but let me check it out," and the rest "Let's go look it up!" As our friend Bart Parrott, a business consultant who returned to medical school at the age of forty, says, "Life is an open-book test."

Going to the library and asking the librarian, or looking in an ency-clopedia, or searching the Internet, or calling a friend in the field, or designing one's own experiment to answer a question—this kind of learning is a hundred times more important than getting the right answers on a test. Learning to answer one's own questions and acquire information is one of the critical tools for becoming truly educated. Or if you can't find the answer? Ask a teacher! Teachers have spent their whole lives preparing to provide information to people who hardly ever ask for it. Teachers generally love to answer questions.

Of course, as with so much in life—especially when it comes to chil-dren—timing and restraint are critical. So don't overdo it. Overan-swering will kill off kids' questioning as surely as refusing to answer. Give them just enough and they'll come back for more.

Michael Soguero: "There's enough curiosity shown by my children that there's plenty to engage with right here in and around our suburban house: reading, plants in the backyard, doing numbers, shopping, etcetera. Whatever we do that's extra is not so much to supplement but part of the life we enjoy and part of interacting with others. This includes farm visits, hands-on science museum, coming with me to work and on retreats with my students, bowl-ing, putt-putt golf, factories (Anderson Pretzels, Crayola), trips into New York City, to Amish Country, to the coal region of Penn-sylvania. . . . "

OPPORTUNITY 101: FINDING SOME FUNDAMENTALS FOR YOU AND YOUR CHILDREN

A list of opportunities—things your family can do to engage intel-lectually in the world of learning—follows. We've covered a number of subject areas, but do not feel you have to do all of these things.

Choose two or three from each category, or simply let our suggestions inspire you to come up with even better ones that suit your family especially well. You may already be participating and engaged in all or many of these areas of cultural, intellectual, and creative life. If this is the case, your participation as a family is shaping and influencing your kids, and that influence is much more important than decontextualized "data-bits" offered by schools.

One caveat: *Don't confuse opportunity with spending money.* Sure, shopping can be fun, and buying some carefully chosen things will help make your kids' world more exciting, but buying is highly overrated as a way to provide your kids with opportunity. In fact, one of the best gifts you can give them is a sense of resourcefulness, of possibility as *distinct* from monetary wealth. "We haven't the money, so we've got to think," said British physicist Lord Rutherford.

For organization's sake, we've divided the world of learning into:

- Books and Literature
- Writing
- Dialogue
- The Arts
- Math and Logic
- Science and Nature
- Community
- The Future

Books and Literature

> Maybe we should declare a 100-year moratorium on the writing of new books, to give everyone a chance to catch up.
> —Writer and radio personality Garrison Keillor

Reading is the single most important skill your kids can learn. It's also one of the primary joys in life, in our view. It doesn't matter what they read. Once they catch the reading bug, they'll keep it for life. Ultimately, if you give or read aloud well-written books, kids will prefer them to poorly written books. It won't take them long to notice the difference. But at first, it's more important to read *anything*. Let books lead to other books, which lead to biographies of the authors, which lead to movies based on the books, which lead to plays. . . . Don't make a big deal about *quality*; the idea is for children to discover the boundless pleasure to be had from reading. You can read out loud; they can listen to books on tape; they can read cookbooks, comic books, or magazines—it doesn't matter. Listening to you read stories, or to books on tape, is literacy; they don't have to be able to read to themselves until they're ready. Literacy is the one fundamental gift you can give your kids that no amount of good schooling will replace and that no amount of poor schooling will diminish. Once they get the hang of reading, the world of learning is open to them forever. Whether your kid's school uses the "whole-language" approach to teaching reading or not, the true whole language shows up in life, not in school. So:

- Read to your kids. Give them books as gifts. Let them see you read. Stock your house with a good basic library—make sure you have a good dictionary, a simple encyclopedia, and a smattering of good fiction and nonfiction written for different ages. Try to have a little bit of everything, but beyond that, go to garage sales, book sales, yard sales, library seconds sales, or bookstores and get random assorted intriguing books. Go to the public library regularly and set aside a special shelf for library books.
- Try to remember what books you loved at your children's ages, and get those for them. Not only will they probably enjoy any book that you remember after all these years, you will enjoy their enjoyment immensely. Or borrow books from older children whom your child admires. Ask your eight-year-old daughter's beloved thirteen-year-old cousin, "What books did you like when you were eight?"
- If your kid is into *Star Wars*, read *Star Wars* books. If your kid is into cartoons, read books about the cartoon characters. X-Men, horses, karate, dinosaurs—it doesn't matter! Just *read*. Eventually the part of the brain that listens instead of watches will click

in and the child will experience the vast, satisfying difference between reading and watching TV.

- Read poetry out loud. Younger children will love Shel Silverstein's hilarious rhyming verse. (see "Opportunity Resources.")
- If you've gotten away from reading for pleasure, get back to it. Or if you've been reading only pulp, escapist fiction and magazines, think about reading some good literature to remind yourself of what education is about. If you've always wanted to/meant to read *The Brothers Karamazov*, or *The Iliad*, or *Bury My Heart at Wounded Knee*, start now. (While writing this book and reading Tolkien's *The Lord of the Rings* to Elijah, Amy began to read Seamus Heaney's new translation of *Beowulf*, and was enchanted to learn that Tolkien's analysis of *Beowulf*'s literary value is still considered definitive—an example of the common, delightful synchronicities that occur in the world of literature. Now she can't wait to find out to what extent *The Lord of the Rings* was inspired by *Beowulf*.)

Writing

> When we left that house and I had to bid my mural goodbye, my mother gave me a notebook in which to note down things I previously had painted: a notebook to record my life. "Here, write what's in your heart," she said. That is what I did then, and that is what I am doing now in these pages. What else can I do?
> —Isabel Allende, *Paula*

People learn to write well not by studying grammar, sentence structure, and spelling but by reading good writing and trying to imitate it. Reading and writing are inextricably linked, and both are symbolic forms of the ancient art of storytelling. Here are some ways to include writing in your lives:

- Write letters. Read the letters you get out loud. Let your prelit-
  erate kids dictate letters or stories to you, and give them a copy.
- Read uncritically what beginning writers produce. They don't
  need correction in spelling or grammar until they're older—
  with Amy's kids, she provides correction only when requested.
  Don't correct everything—choose one issue (spelling, contrac-
  tions) at a time.
- Play Scrabble, Boggle, Mad Libs, and other word games. Let
  beginning readers spell words any way they want; later you can
  get more picky. Games are a great way to provide a place for kids
  to practice language skills without noticing it. Amy invented a
  treasure hunt game for Elijah when he was first beginning to
  read—each of the clues is composed of words that Elijah knows
  on sight or can easily decipher. As Elijah eagerly read the clues
  (which Amy tried to make funny, as in "look on the potty"), he
  usually failed to notice that he was reading at all. The game built
  on Elijah's strengths and skills, involved his whole body (he's a
  strongly kinesthetic learner), and had a purpose (finding the
  treasure) beyond practicing the skill for its own sake.
- Keep a journal, and give your kids journals.
- Try writing funny songs or poems as a family.
- Buy or make poetry refrigerator magnets. They're great for all
  ages and deliver a lot of bang for the buck.
- Listen to and discuss the lyrics of kids' favorite songs. Think
  about why a particular lyric is moving. If you object to a lyric, be
  prepared to say why thoughtfully and to compare it with examples of controversial popular art from your own youth.
- Discuss other kinds of writing that interest or move you. Why are
  the Harry Potter books so fascinating? Why do you prefer one
  magazine over another?
- Give kids their own writing supplies—*Kids Have All the Write Stuff*,
  by Sharon A. Edwards and Robert W. Maloy (see "Opportunity
  Resources") suggests a special writing box for each child, with
  paper, markers, pencils, and other inviting tools.
- Attend writing conferences, classes, or groups.
- Go hear writers speak or read at bookstores.
- If you've always wanted to write, start now. Excellent books on writ-

ing for adults and older teens are *If You Want to Write* by Brenda Ueland and *Writing Down the Bones* by Natalie Goldberg. These books encourage the reader to write clearly and from the heart (see "Opportunity Resources" for these and other books on writing).

- Stock your resource shelf with Strunk and White's *The Elements of Style* and *Fowler's Modern English Usage* (or *Modern American Usage*). These two witty, elegant, and simple volumes are worth many times their weight in boring English textbooks.

Dialogue

> At his Table [my father] lik'd to have as often as he could, some sensible Friend or Neighbour, to converse with, and always took care to start some ingenious or useful Topic for Discourse, which might tend to improve the Minds of his Children. By this means he turn'd our Attention to what was good, just, & prudent in the Conduct of Life; and little or no Notice was ever taken of what related to the Victuals on the Table. . . .
>
> —Benjamin Franklin, *Autobiography*

Teach your children to listen carefully and to speak thoughtfully. The best way to teach this is to listen carefully and speak thoughtfully to your children, from the time they're babies. It's never too late to begin this practice. Take their questions and ideas seriously. Although most people may not associate doing so immediately with education, learning to speak and listen as if our words matter is fundamental to it. Dialogue is not the same as mindless chatter. Include your kids in serious and philosophical conversations throughout their childhoods and adolescence. Invite interesting guests to your home, and include your kids in those conversations. Strike up conversations with interesting strangers when you're shopping or traveling. Above all, *listen, listen,* and *listen* to your kids.

- If it works in your lives, make a practice of inviting interesting people to dinner regularly, or have regular potlucks. Grace fondly recalls living for two of her college years at "Farm House," a natural history–interest house where the fourteen residents shared dinners each night and not only allowed each other to invite guests but encouraged each other to do so—in fact, occasionally at their weekly house meetings, someone would complain: "We haven't had enough guests lately." They viewed these guests as opportunities, and took it upon themselves to invite not only friends but professors, interesting people they'd met in town, and visiting speakers. (One night National Book Award winner Barry Lopez joined them for dinner, an experience Grace found unforgettable.) They'd start each meal with a round of introductions, and conversation was lively and inspiring.

- If you've always wanted to initiate more meaningful conversations, express yourself more completely, and talk more often about things that interest you, start now.

- Provide a place for your kids to be involved in *philosophical* discussions—where people talk about the nature of things. Teenagers especially begin to search earnestly for meaning in life, and exposure to intellectual inquiry or different models can tempt them away from more dangerous kinds of exploration. Talk around your dinner table, or help kids set up a peer study group. Ask them big questions, such as what they think about why things are the way they are. Make sure to be a model of open-mindedness and curiosity, taking on different perspectives, trying on different ideas, demonstrating your ability to be flexible, and exploring rather than sticking to one particular viewpoint. "Well, the Stoics said life was like this; my uncle Louis said life is like that—what do *you* think?" Encourage them to consider: What are the implications of adopting a particular viewpoint? How would that affect the way you live your life? How would that influence you to behave or experience the world? Consider the perspective that all these different viewpoints are just stories we tell ourselves; that ultimately the test of their truth may lie in their implication for how we choose to live. Or is there another kind of truth?

The Arts

Beauty heals us, surprises us, encourages us, and frees us.
—Irish theologian John O'Donohue, *The Divine Imagination*

Although they are often treated as frivolous, pleasant "extras" in public schools, the arts are central to the development of an intellectually vital, self-expressed, satisfied human being. Julia Cameron's books (*The Artist's Way* and others; see "Opportunity Resources") are marvelous guides to finding and encouraging your own creative expression as a path to fulfillment and spiritual connection. In fact, *Artist's Way* groups have sprung up around the country where people share their experience of reading the book and doing the exercises. So consider an *Artist's Way* group for your family! If you've always wanted to take up watercolor painting or tap-dancing, or fantasized about having just an itsy-bitsy part in a community musical production, perhaps now's the time.

- Visit art museums, galleries, and arts centers. (Many cities have cooperative studio space where you can see artists at work as well as view their work.)
- Check out coffee-table books about different artists at the library.
- Keep art supplies available in the house at all times—don't expect children to learn and engage in the visual arts only at school.
- Depending on the resources where you live, and where your own and your kids' passions lie, explore architecture, textile design, filmmaking, jewelry making, stained glass, statues in the park, photography . . .
- Sing songs and rounds as a family.
- Sing and play music to your children.
- Offer your children music lessons if you can afford it. If not, offer

your children classes through school, or ask a musician friend to help them learn. Or teach yourself from a book or video, and invite your child to learn along with you.

- Offer to take kids to different kinds of concerts so they can hear live music and see the people who make it.
- Have instruments in your house—drums, rattles made of split peas, tone drums, old guitars picked up from yard sales. (Or see Bart Hopkin's *Making Simple Musical Instruments*, in "Opportunity Resources.")
- Put music on the stereo and have whole-family dances.
- Go dancing—Sufi dancing, square dancing, swing dancing, whatever—as a family.
- Go see dance performances by both kids and professionals.
- Get familiar with your local paper's "upcoming events" section and schedule outings to dramatic events to see if your family enjoys theater.
- Attend plays, concerts, and performance art offered inexpensively or free. These are often available even in small towns. (One advantage of seeing local theater instead of big expensive shows, besides the price, is that if your kids get interested, they probably can get involved in the company.)
- Encourage your children to write and produce a play at home— which their family and friends can then attend.
- Play charades as a family.

Math and Logic

When we think of math and young children, most of us think mainly in terms of arithmetic, flash cards, and trying to invent fun drills to help kids memorize the multiplication tables. Giving kids—young or not so young—access to math can be so much broader. As Patricia Kenschaft says in her wonderful book, *Math Power: How to Help Your Child Love Math, Even if You Don't:* "Computation (routine calculation) is to mathematics as spelling is to literature. It has value in itself, but it is no substitute for the real thing." (See "Opportunity Resources.") Just as we'd make a dreary mistake by emphasizing spelling and not reading at all to our kids or introducing them to great books, so also we do them a disservice when we stress arithmetic at the expense of broader mathematical thinking. The problem is, many of us are clueless, fearful, and incompetent when it comes to math—and it's no wonder, because our own parents, and our teachers, passed along to us their fear and confusion. But even if you come from a long line of mathophobes, you can choose to break the cycle and help your kids feel comfortable in mathematical terrain.

In one of our favorite books of all time, *How Children Fail*, author John Holt writes:

> The more we can make it possible for children to see how we use numbers, *and to use them as we use them*, the better. What do we adults do with numbers? We measure things with them, a huge variety of things in the real world around us. Why? So that we can think better about them and make better use of them. We measure, among a host of other reasons, to find out whether we are sick or well; to find out whether we are doing something better than we did before; to find out which of several ways of doing this is better; to find out how strong we have to make things in order to make them stand up; to find out where we are, or where we're going; to find out, if we do a certain thing, what other things are likely to happen as a result. And so on. We don't measure things out of idle curiosity. We measure them *so that we can decide things about them and do things with them*. . . . So we should introduce children to numbers by giving them or making available to them as many measuring instruments as possible—rulers, measuring tapes (in both feet and meters), scales, watches and stop-watches, thermometers, metronomes, barometers, light meters, decibel meters, and so on. Whatever we measure in our lives and work, we should try to measure so that children can see us doing it, and we should try to make it possible for them to measure the same things, and let them know how we are thinking about the things we have measured.[1]

---

[1] John Holt, *How Children Fail* (Reading, MA: Addison-Wesley, 1982), pp. 222–223.

Here are some more specific possibilities for giving kids math opportunities:

- Give kids an allowance. Encourage them to save a certain amount in an interest-bearing account.
- Play logic games like chess, Mastermind, and Go.
- Talk with children openly and unmelodramatically about your own math fears.
- Pick up a book like Harold Jacobs's *Math: A Human Endeavor,* Charles Seiter's *Everyday Math for Dummies,* or Stephen Slavin's *All the Math You'll Ever Need* (see "Opportunity Resources"). Start working through it yourself and then (naturally) incorporating your new or restored knowledge into your everyday activities and speech.
- Introduce kids to logic puzzles—which develop high-level math thinking skills without much use of numbers and are therefore excellent exercises for people who are uncomfortable with arithmetic.
- Let kids help with grocery shopping (including decision making).
- Let them help you plan a budget for their clothing.
- Get them copies of the *Schoolhouse Rock* videos.
- Help them set up a simple home business in which you hire them to provide services like recycling or coupon clipping (for financial benefit to both of you). (For excellent ideas in this department, see "Opportunity Resources" for Adriane Berg and Arthur Bochner's *Totally Awesome Business Book for Kids.*)
- Give them some money to invest. (Again, see "Opportunity Resources" for Adriane Berg and Arthur Bochner's *Totally Awesome Money Book for Kids and Their Parents.*)
- Bake with them, doubling or halving a recipe.
- Let them see you using arithmetic, algebra, or geometry to achieve your own goals.
- Sometimes in conversations, draw simple graphs to illustrate your points, and encourage them to do the same.

Science and Nature

> As a working hypothesis to explain the riddle of our existence, I pro-
> pose that our universe is the most interesting of all possible universes,
> and our fate as human beings is to make it so.
> —Freeman Dyson, *Infinite in All Directions*

Science education can be roughly divided into two parts: There's "what science knows"—the body of data and information that's been accumulated during the past several thousand years of systematic scientific inquiry into our world—and there's "how science works"—the tools and methods scientists use to gain that information in the various fields. Kids, who naturally apply the scientific method to researching life from the day they are born, love learning about both. Schools have a tendency to suck the joy out of science by focusing on rote memorization of no-context facts. You can counteract that sucking action by encouraging your children's natural wonder, questioning, exploring, and research.

The Natural World

> Hands-on experience at the critical time, not systematic knowledge, is
> what counts in the making of a naturalist. Better to be an untutored
> savage for a while, not to know the names or anatomical detail. Better
> to spend long stretches of time just searching and dreaming.
> —Edward O. Wilson, *Naturalist*

If you are lucky enough to live in an area with access to nature—even if it's just a small wood at the end of your street—encourage kids to get out in it. Go there with them. Children innately have enormous powers of observation. Pay attention to what they notice and observe. You don't have to turn everything into an academic exercise, but if you feel so guided, one fun and productive possibility even for fairly young children is to take along a notebook and sketch intriguing insects, plants, or animals. Amy's family (who live in the countryside) uses a "nature notebook" to record all interesting events, including the date, time, and place observed. Some of the exciting listings in the notebook over many years are five bald eagle sightings, one sighting of a (still-unidentified) flaming object in the sky in broad daylight, and the appearance after a spring flood of mysterious transparent shrimplike creatures in a neighbor's backyard. (You'll find the mystery solved on page 162.) Our friend Tina and her ten-year-old daughter, Anna, are identifying moths this summer under the porch light at their house in the woods, using a field guide. If no natural area is easily accessible to your children at home, try finding a city garden plot to visit, or take regular trips to your city's arboretum, botanical gardens, or parks. The emotional and spiritual gifts children receive from connecting regularly with nature are incalculable, even apart from the educational value.

- Get inexpensive field guides to the flora, fauna, and geology of your area.
- Go on walks with your kids to nearby semiwild areas—an irrigation ditch bank, or a grove of trees at the edge of your suburb, or just through alleyways where you can hear more birds or look at insects together.
- Read or check out photography books and magazines from the library. Try Ansel Adams, sculptor/photographer Andy Goldsworthy, or *National Geographic*.
- Even if you're not campers, you may still want to design a low-stress camping trip for your family. Ask friends who are experts to help you out, or camp out in the backyard.
- Buy an inexpensive camera—35mm cameras are available for under ten dollars—and let your child take photographs of her discoveries. You can find inexpensive film developing at your local grocery or drugstore.

Amy: Elijah, like so many young children, has always been fascinated with dinosaurs, choosing to read nonfiction books about dinosaurs at bedtime year after year. Before the Disney movie *Dinosaur* came out, Elijah chose to rent the video *Tarzan* twice just so he could see the preview for *Dinosaur!* The question of how the dinosaurs died out especially intrigues him, including the idea that science has not conclusively answered that question. ("Was it a comet or a meteor that killed the dinosaurs? What's the difference? If a comet's made of ice, what happens if it hits the sun? How big was it? Where did it fall? Will a comet ever hit Earth again? How often do they fall?. . . . " Phew, I'm researching as fast as I can.) Recently I came across newspaper reports that a fossilized dinosaur heart had been discovered, the structure of which lends evidence to the emerging theory that the dinosaurs were not cold-blooded like reptiles but warm-blooded like mammals and birds. Both Elijah and Carsie were thrilled and astounded to hear the news, shared at the breakfast table. Carsie wanted to know how a heart—soft tissue—could be fossilized. (The newspaper article provided the answer.) Elijah wanted to know if amphibians were warm-blooded. (Carsie told him no, and referred him to his salamander collection.) Carsie and I discussed some differences between warm- and cold-blooded creatures and what the implications for dinosaur behavior might be if they indeed were warm-blooded. Carsie, who has also been fascinated by biology since she was small, speculated that perhaps the dinosaurs actually nursed their babies like egg-laying mammals do. That hypothesis—which I have never heard proposed before—remains to be explored.

- Try talking at lunch or dinner about where each part of your meal comes from.
- If you have a yard, turn a portion of it into a haven for wildlife, native plants, birds, or butterflies.
- Help your child make a terrarium in an old aquarium. (You can find aquariums at yard sales, but you have to get there early.) Put a few inches of soil in it and dig up and plant some small plants. Sink a shallow dish into the soil for a pond. Give the child responsibility for keeping the terrarium watered. When she

finds interesting insects, frogs, tadpoles, salamanders, lizards, turtles, or spiders, she can add them to the aquarium. Amy's family keeps found reptiles and amphibians for a week or so and then releases them back to nature. (For some creatures, you'll want to make sure the lid fits tightly!)

- Start gardening, and offer kids their own little plot. Many cities provide community gardening plots for families without their own yards.
- Find ways to let kids see you comfortable and happy in the natural world.

The Physical Sciences

> I would sometimes beg my mother to bring out her engagement ring and show me the diamond in it. It flashed like nothing I had ever seen, almost as if it gave out more light than it took in. My mother showed me how easily it scratched glass, and then she told me to put it to my lips. It was strangely, startlingly cold—metals felt cool to the touch, but the diamond was icy. That was because it conducted heat so well, she said—better than any metal—so it drew the body heat away from one's lips when they touched it. This was a feeling I was never to forget. Another time, she showed me how if one touched a diamond to a cube of ice it would draw heat from one's hand into the ice and cut straight through it as if it were butter.
>
> —Neurologist Oliver Sachs, *Brilliant Light*

As we suggested earlier in the chapter, take children's wondering seriously and engage in it with them. Ask questions together—why is the sky blue? Where do the frogs go in the wintertime? How do airplanes fly? Design experiments at home. Get in the habit of researching the answers to kids'—and your—questions. If you have access to the Internet, research is often fast and simple. Once you get into a subject area, you may want to go to museum exhibits dealing with it, or clip out newspaper articles. As an added bonus (for the teacher too), your kids will be enthusiastic participants when they study the subject in school.

Here are some ways that you can inspire your children to learn more about the miracle of our physical world:

- Stock up on science experiment books, simple equipment like graph paper, a simple microscope, a hand lens.
- A powerful pair of binoculars can be useful for beginning astronomers (often more so than a cheap telescope) and also can facilitate birdwatching.
- Some newspapers include astronomy news, which discusses what's going on in the night sky. Amy's kids particularly love the meteor showers in August and November. On clear nights, everyone lies down on the roof in sleeping bags waiting to see how many shooting stars they can see before falling asleep. One night it was so clear that the falling stars cast shadows on the walls of the kids' bedrooms. There are also Web sites that offer up-to-date astronomical information. (See "Opportunity Resources.")
- Brush up on how the standard scientific method works: Ask a question, form a hypothesis, test it, adjust your hypothesis and test it again, and eventually make a theory based on your results.
- If you don't remember or didn't learn the basics of biology, astrology, physics, geology, or chemistry in school, you may enjoy reading simple science books written for laypeople. People who found science painful and boring in school often find it fascinating and accessible as adults, when their curiosity about the world reawakens. As you rediscover the joys of understanding our world in a rational, systematic way, your enthusiasm will inevitably spill over to your kids.
- If your kids are into dinosaurs or other archeological matters, find out if there's a dig happening nearby. Your local university's archeology department will know if the dig is open to the public. At some ongoing digs, the public is invited to help.
- Get anatomy charts. Ask about free posters at your doctor's office or clinic. Learn about the makeup of your own bodies together.
- Choose a small space in your house to transform into a cornucopia

of science inspiration. Stock a coffee table or bathroom shelf with a changing array of books from your shelves or the library.

- Cover hallway walls with inviting, informative charts, maps, or posters—about dinosaurs, the phases of the moon, the wild-flowers of your region. If you live in the country, see if your local agricultural extension office has free posters.

- Or fill a mantelpiece—or a bowl in the middle of the dining room table—full of rocks, minerals, feathers, acorns, shells, fos-sils, and other natural objects—treasures from your camping trips, walks, or explorations.

Technology and the Internet

The federal government is currently pouring money into America's schools to make sure every classroom has at least one computer and Internet access. This effort attempts to ensure fairness in computer literacy, so that poor districts have a chance at the same kind of technology that prosperous districts can obtain. Yet while computer literacy will be increasingly important in years to come, such literacy is obtained essentially through the use of basic reading skills. In other words, if children learn to read well, they will be able to use the Internet later on, even if they don't have access to a computer at a young age. Also, there is little research to support the idea that using computers as a primary tool for learning subjects other than the computers themselves is justified. So while we're glad that poor children are going to have access to computer technology, don't for-

---

Amy: When she was ten, Carsie read an article about NAFTA (the North American Free Trade Agreement) for school and told me of her strong feelings against it. I encouraged her to write our representative and showed her how to find his office address. She wrote a letter and received a personal response, signed by Congressman Wolf, thanking her for her comments. She was very proud of that letter. Later we attended a local meeting at which the congressman was present, and she spoke to him. She has a strong sense of justice and of her ability to make an impact on the world.

get that people educated themselves for hundreds of years *without* computers.

Still, if you live in one of the 50 percent of American households connected to the Internet, your children *do* have access to one more resource for information and connection to other people. Because the Internet is an easily available forum for any ideas, children need adult wisdom and guidance concerning how to take advantage of the resource, how to find useful information, and how to distinguish propaganda, advertising, and smut from the good stuff. We've included a short list of Web sites we find helpful in the "Opportunity Resources" section of this chapter. In addition to offering Internet availability to your children, consider giving them:

- Books on technology
- Old stuff (phones, toasters, computers) to take apart and put back together
- Pieces of computers so they can build their own
- Software that teaches computer programming languages
- The Transtech catalog
- Magazines about cutting-edge technology, such as *Popular Science*

Community

> This summer I am working on a project to record the history of [the town of] Idlewild as told by the people who lived it. It involves talking to elderly people and videotaping, and is paid for by a job training program funded by the school district. I spend at least three hours each day at the local meals program in Baldwin. Old timers come to spend time with their friends and eat. They tell me about Idlewild in the fifties. I find it fascinating hearing their stories. I like to listen to the elderly talk to each other about growing up in the days of big families, home grown food, and even homeschooling! One lady told me that when she was growing up there was no school to go to. They were taught arithmetic, reading, and writing at home by mothers, fathers, grandparents, aunts, uncles, and any other adult around. They tell me if I stick around they will learn *me* something. They also tell me that it is a good thing, what I am doing. And they say I should talk to some really old people before they die or forget what they know.
>
> —fifteen-year-old Ayanna Williams *in Real Lives: Eleven Teenagers Who Don't Go to School* (edited by Grace Llewellyn)

The more children are included in the living, vital, tangible life of their community, the more the abstract concepts of politics, history, and cultural studies will come alive for them. Remember that it's never too early to begin involving your children in a wider view of the society of which your family is a part.

The Political Process

Include your kids in local political processes, so they can see how individuals have an effect (even if they just involve your local food co-op board meetings and neighborhood associations). Let kids participate in, and witness, different kinds of decision-making processes—voting, consensus, hierarchy (bosses), and so on. And talk with them about governmental elections, your feelings about different candidates, your feelings about the process itself.

- Encourage your kids to write letters to your representatives when they feel strongly about a political issue.
- Keep up with important issues and involve your kids in discussions about them.
- Experiment in your own household. While you wouldn't do your kids a favor by pretending that your family is a democracy, you could designate certain types of decisions as "voting decisions" or "consensus decisions," and then experiment with these processes together.

Different Cultures/Walks of Life

Travel and exposure to different cultures not only broadens our understanding of other people's lives but of our own. Sometimes the best way to understand one's own culture is to leave it temporarily.

- Watch movies set in different countries, especially ones made by directors and actors from those countries.
- Read stories and memoirs of different cultures.

- Stretch yourself by inviting people not in your regular circles to dinner.
- Visit neighborhoods and attend festivals of other ethnicities.
- If your child's schoolmates include children of different nations and cultures, encourage your child to learn about them. Check out library books set in those countries, try preparing their food at home, and research famous Americans with similar heritage.
- Some areas are served by cable channels that specialize in broadcasting TV shows from other countries: the daily news from France, a soccer match from Bolivia, and so on.
- Join travel organizations like Servas, an international network of hosts who welcome travellers of all races and cultural backgrounds in their homes, as well as travellers who are interested in participating in the daily life of their host families (see "Opportunity Resources" at the end of this chapter).

History

> Biography is the only true history.
> —British historian and essayist Thomas Carlyle

Kathleen Phillips, a Spanish teacher and mother of two daughters who are now twelve and fourteen, writes: "When the girls were two and four years old, my husband and I took them to Guatemala to live with a family while I studied Spanish for three weeks for eight hours a day. Last year we all went to Mexico while I went to school for two weeks. I feel these trips are one of the most valuable educational opportunities that we offer our children and ourselves. We have had foreign exchange students and foreign exchange teachers in our home for six years, and two Japanese summer exchange students. I feel this is also one of the more valuable educational experiences. We don't have to talk about culture; the children experience it firsthand and can discuss live experiences rather than book experiences. Olivia, our youngest, says she wants to be an exchange student some day in a Spanish-speaking country."

Of all the academic areas, history may be the one most transformed by being vividly related to one's present life. History is not dry facts and remote events but the stories we tell ourselves about human experience, no matter how vast or slight the scale. Anything that brings these stories alive for children will help prepare them to understand and remember history as they grow.

- Search out good historical fiction, films, and well-written history books.
- Tell stories from your own life and from the lives of your parents and grandparents. Around the dinner table or at family gatherings, invite your kids to tell stories too: "Heather, will you tell about the time we adopted the baby skunks?"
- David Weitzman's *My Backyard History Book* (see "Opportunity Resources") is great for kids ages about eight to twelve; it offers activities that bridge the gap between the reader and human history. (For instance, it asks the reader to analyze her or his own name, then to make a personal time line, a birthday time machine . . . and then to branch out and make a family tree, collect family stories and photos . . . and then further out to inves-

---

Aubyn Burnside, thirteen, from Hickory, North Carolina, founded "Suitcases for Kids," a program that collects and distributes used suitcases for children in foster care. When Aubyn was seven, she learned that kids being moved from one foster home to another usually have to carry their belongings in trash bags. "I thought, 'That is horrible. These children must feel like garbage!'" Aubyn reports. She conceived a project to ensure that every child in foster care would have a suitcase of his or her own. Publicizing her project through local newspapers and in her Girl Scouts and 4-H newsletters, and collecting used suitcases at yard sales, Aubyn started small. The donations and the message grew, and soon she was speaking at state-wide conferences on her program and passing out starter kits for other groups to launch Suitcases for Kids programs in their areas. Because nearly 4,500 suitcases have been donated so far, Aubyn is now enlisting support from trucking companies to transport the excess to areas in need.

tigate history in antique shops, cemeteries, by looking at old
buildings, etc.)

- Encourage kids to keep logs or journals of family trips.
- Immerse your family in the study of a period in history if interest leads you there. Seek out films, museums, books, songs, and
  people related to that time. Visit reenactments or living history
  museums. Virginia is blessed with world-class resources: the living historical village of Colonial Williamsburg (expensive); the
  excellent Frontier Museum of American History (inexpensive),
  which has four working farms from different cultures and periods of time; and plenty of Civil War battle reenactments (free,
  but earplugs required!). The annual Maryland Renaissance Fair
  and the Harlem Renaissance Fair in D.C. are easy day trips. Every
  state has its own wealth of living history if you look for it. Does
  Amy take her kids out of school to attend these activities when
  convenient? You bet.

Foreign Language

In many schools, children are not exposed to foreign languages until
adolescence. Yet young children have an easier time learning languages and mimicking accents. Your family might choose one foreign
language for adults and children to study together, giving you a built-
in practice group. Other ways to practice:

- Rent foreign videos, and watch them several times to try to catch
  more of the language on each pass.
- Hang out in Chinatown or other neighborhoods where people
  speak languages other than English.
- Consider hosting an exchange student, and help your children
  explore the possibility of being exchange students.
- If your children have a non–English-speaking friend or baby-
  sitter, encourage the friend to speak to them in his or her native
  language. Amy practiced her high school French in conversations with her best friend's family, Haitians who spoke a beautiful, lightly accented French in their home.

The Future

A few years back a famous school at Harvard issued some advice to its own students on planning a career in the new economy it believes is arriving. It warned sharply that academic classes and professional credentials would begin to count for less and less when measured against real world training . . . for what it's worth I'm going to pass on the nine qualities that the Harvard department thought would be essential to finding a place in the new world order:

1) The ability to define problems without a guide.
2) The ability to ask hard questions challenging prevailing assumptions.
3) The ability to pull out what is needed from masses of irrelevant information.
4) The ability to work in teams without guidance. .
5) The ability to work alone.
6) The ability to persuade others that your course is right.
7) The ability to make new patterns with old information.
8) The ability to present, discuss and debate in public.
9) The ability to think inductively, deductively, dialectically, and heuristically.[2]

—John Gatto, *Homefires* magazine

 At the heart of Opportunity is: ENGAGEMENT. Stay passionate, involved, and interested in life and in learning. Your enthusiasm will transfer automatically to your kids.

Opportunity Exercises

For you:

1. Make a list of learning opportunities you'd like to bring into your life, just for yourself. Your list can be long or short, one item or six pages—the point is to open yourself up to new possibilities for learning, discovery, and engagement.

2. Now see if there are any items on your list that you're ready to pursue. You're not committing to doing these things, just to exploring or obtaining the necessary resources so that the opportunity is readily available.

For your kids:

1. As a family, make a list of learning opportunities that you or other family members would like to add to your lives. Use our list as a jumping-off point if you like. Let people fantasize freely at first—this is about possibility, not practicality!

2. Once you have an exciting list of possibilities, further refine it and agree on the things to which you're willing to commit time and energy. Again, you needn't commit to *doing* these things—for instance, agreeing to rent a Spanish movie or go to a Mexican restaurant is not a commitment to learn Spanish. Opportunity is about not only involvement but exploration.

Guerrilla Learning as a whole is based on the idea that real education leads people to the ability to think and to act and speak thoughtfully, which encompasses these higher-order skills reportedly needed in the new economy. (We happen to think that these skills were needed in the old world order too, but never mind.) We want our kids to learn not what to think but *how* to think. One way to increase your children's chances of developing these skills is to give them (or allow them) real projects, not academic exercises, where an outcome in the real world is intended and where the *result*, not the assessment of an authority, is the ultimate judge of the project's success.

- Help your kids set long- and short-term goals, and evaluate their own progress toward those goals.
- Encourage and allow kids to dream up projects, large and small. Take their projects seriously. They may learn more of the life

skills they eventually will need by doing projects of their own design than by doing school-assigned busywork.

- Take your children, of both genders, to work with you, even when it's not "Take Your Daughter to Work Day."
- Help your kids get familiar and comfortable with what's possible. We have to understand not only that wonderful things—stars, Baroque music, digital photography—exist, but that they could be ours. Several ways to help your kids understand this, in their bones, are to:

  - Be a role model and let your kids see other adult role models who understand how to reach for their dreams.
  - Talk with your kids in a way that helps them see their own possibilities.
  - Provide a small taste of, or a way for them to participate briefly in, something that interests them.
  - Provide an immersion experience.

Parents have a great deal of power to influence their kids in the realm of the future. If there's something you hope they'll get interested in and become good at, you can help them feel comfortable with it—numbers, foreign language, reading, whatever. Share your fantasies about your kids' futures in a low-key, unattached, friendly, and nonsecretive ways.

- Let children see you and other adults in action. Opportunity consists of anything that gives a human being more of a sense of possibility, especially a sense of *delightful* possibility. As your kids' strongest link to the adult world, you, therefore, do them a great service by happily tinkering away at whatever you like to do, right under their noses. And make mistakes, wonder out loud, choose gorgeously large goals for yourself and attempt valiantly to reach them, pursue questions big and small . . . engage in much of this in the family room, at the dinner table, or on the telephone within earshot.
- Use "Powerful possible talk." Tell your kids that whatever they see out in the world—something people are doing, or just some

thing—like ocean waves or airplanes—if they feel drawn to it, there's a way for them to make it theirs. As adults we tend to forget how limited a child's thinking can be. So it's not that you should say to your kid every time you see his eyes dart at someone doing something, "Would you like to do that?" But do tell him frequently that anything he's interested in has many openings, or doorways, or tunnels, or windows, through which he can approach it. Sometimes say specifically what those openings or tunnels might be. If your son is enthralled by frogs, you could tell him that you could take him camping, or on a picnic, near a pond full of frogs. Or he could watch a TV special on frogs, spend more time at the local frog pond, or start a naturalist's journal with sketches and field notes. Or read or look at books, create a frog habitat in your own backyard, find Web sites or Internet newsgroups, start a club to raise awareness about the alarming disappearance of frogs from the environment, or set up an aquarium and keep frogs as pets (or keep tadpoles until they turn into frogs). You could arrange for a biology student or a professional naturalist to accompany him to a froggy site and to talk with him about frogs' lives. You get the idea.

- Ask neighbors and friends to convey the sense of their work to your kids and perhaps to take them to work as well.
- Help older children research potential paths to careers and to explore how their gifts can be translated into different kinds of jobs.

Opportunity Resources

Books, Literature, and Writing

Adler, Mortimer, and Charles Van Doren. *How to Read a Book*. New York: Simon and Schuster, 1972.

Edwards, Sharon A., and Robert W. Maloy. *Kids Have All the Write Stuff: Inspiring Your Children to Put Pencil* to Paper (*Or Crayon, or Felt-Tip Marker, or Computer)*. New York: Penguin, 1992.

Goldberg, Natalie. *Writing Down the Bones: Freeing the Writer Within.* Boston: Shambhala, 1986.

Klauser, Henriette Anne. *Put Your Heart on Paper.* New York: Bantam, 1995.

Sheffer, Susannah. *Writing Because We Love To: Homeschoolers at Work.* Portsmouth, NH: Heinemann, 1992.

Silverstein, Shel. *A Light in the Attic.* New York: HarperCollins, 1981.

———. *Where the Sidewalk Ends : The Poems and Drawings of Shel Silverstein.* New York: HarperCollins, 1974.

Stillman, Peter. *Families Writing.* Cincinnati: Writer's Digest, 1998.

———. *Write Away : A Friendly Guide for Teenage Writers.* Portsmouth, NH: Heinemann, 1995.

Ueland, Brenda. *If You Want to Write: A Book About Art, Independence, and Spirit.* St. Paul, MN: Graywolf Press, 1997.

Williams, Jane. *Stocking a Home Library Inexpensively.* Shingle Springs, CA: Bluestocking, 1995.

Also see the "Keeping Kids Reading" Web site (www.tiac.net/users/maryl).

Dialogue

Faber, Adele, and Elaine Mazlish. *How to Talk So Kids Will Listen and Listen So Kids Will Talk.* New York: Avon, 1999.

Gaarder, Jostein. *Sophie's World : A Novel About the History of Philosophy.* New York: Berkley, 1996.

The Arts

Music for Little People Catalog, P.O. Box 1460, Redway, CA 95560, 1-800-346-4445, musicforlittlepeople.com.

Cameron, Julia. *The Artist's Way.* New York: Tarcher, 1992.

Hopkin, Bart. *Making Simple Musical Instruments: A Melodious Collection of Strings, Winds, Drums & More.* New York: Sterling: 1999.

Judy, Stephanie. *Making Music for the Joy of It.* New York: Tarcher, 1990.

Warner, Sally. *Encouraging the Artist in Your Child.* New York: St. Martin's Press, 1989.

Math and Logic

Berg, Adriane, and Arthur Bochner. *The Totally Awesome Business Book for Kids.* New York: Newmarket, 1995.

————. *The Totally Awesome Money Book for Kids and Their Parents.* New York: Newmarket, 1997.

Burns, Marilyn. *The I Hate Mathematics Book.* Boston: Little, Brown, 1976.

Jacobs, Harold. *Math: A Human Endeavor,* 3rd ed. New York: W. H. Freeman, 1994.

Kenschaft, Patricia. *Math Power: How to Help Your Child Love Math, Even if You Don't.* Reading, MA: Perseus, 1997.

Pappas, Theoni. *The Joy of Mathematics.* San Carlos, CA: Tetra, 1989.

Rucker, Rudy. *Mind Tools: The Five Levels of Mathematical Reality.* Boston: Houghton Mifflin, 1988.

Seiter, Charles. *Everyday Math for Dummies.* Foster City, CA: IDG, 1995.

Sheffer, Susannah, ed. *Unschooling Math.* Cambridge, MA: Holt Associates, 1995.

Slavin, Stephen L. *All the Math You'll Ever Need : A Self-Teaching Guide,* revised edition. New York: John Wiley & Sons, 1999.

Stewart, Ian. *Nature's Numbers: The Unreal Reality of Mathematics.* New York: Basic Books, 1997.

Science and Nature

Allison, Linda. *Blood and Guts: A Working Guide to Your Own Insides.* Boston: Little, Brown, 1976.

Beres, Samantha. *101 Things Every Kid Should Know About Science.* Lincolnwood, IL: Lowell House, 1998.

Cornell, Joseph. *Sharing Nature With Children.* Nevada City, CA: Dawn, 1998

Ontario Science Center. *Scienceworks.* Reading, MA: Addison-Wesley, 1986.

Tiner, John Hudson. *100 Scientists Who Shaped World History.* San Mateo, CA: Bluewood Books, 2000.

Vancleave, Janice Pratt. *Science for Every Kid* (series). New York: John Wiley & Sons.

Wollard, Kathy. *How Come? Every Kid's Science Questions Explained.* New York: Workman, 1993.

See *Sky & Telescope Magazine's* Web site, www.skypub.com, for information on current events in the night sky. Also the NASA Observatorium site —www.ivv.nasa.gov—a public access site for earth and space data.

Community

Carey, John. ed. *Eyewitness to History*. New York: Avon, 1997.

Copsey, Susan Elizabeth, Barnabas Kindersley, Anabel Kindersley, and Harry Belafonte. *Children Just Like Me*. New York: DK Publishing, 1995.

Fernandez-Armesto, Felipe. *Millennium: A History of the Last Thousand Years*. New York: Touchstone, 1996.

Gastil, John. *Democracy in Small Groups*. Stoney Creek, CT: New Society Publishers, 1993.

Goldstein, Richard, ed. *Mine Eyes Have Seen: A First-Person History of the Events That Shaped America*. New York: Touchstone, 1997.

Hakim, Joy. *A History of US*, revised. New York: Oxford University Press, 1999.

Jeffrey, Nan. *Adventuring With Children: An Inspirational Guide to World Travel and the Outdoors*. Ashland, MA: Avalon House, 1995.

Servas, www.servas.org

Weitzman, David. *My Backyard History Book*. Boston: Little, Brown, 1975.

General

Brand, Stewart, and Peter Warshall, eds. *The Original Whole Earth Catalog, Special 30th Anniversary Issue*. Sansalito, CA: Whole Earth, 1998.

Kealoha, Anna. *Trust the Children: A Manual and Activity Guide for Home-schooling and Alternative Learning*. Berkeley, CA: Celestial Arts, 1995.

Reed, Donn. *The Home School Source Book*. Bridgewater, ME: Brook Farms Books, 1994.

Rupp, Rebecca. *Complete Home Learning Sourcebook: The Essential Resource Guide for Homeschoolers, Parents, and Educators*. New York: Three Rivers Press, 1998.

Stock, Gregory. *The Book of Questions*. New York: Workman, 1987.

Stock, Gregory. *The Kids' Book of Questions*. New York: Workman, 1988.

Two excellent encyclopedias are now on-line for free: www.britanica.com

and www.grolier.com. The price: you have to put up with advertising (if you want ad-free access, you have to pay). The advantages over old-fashioned hard-bound volumes: dynamic cross-referencing, multimedia presentations, and continuous updating.

Also free on-line are www.thesaurus.com and www.dictionary.com.

The Education Source (www.edusource.com) lists dozens of education-related Web sites including homework help sites, search engines for kids, and information on on-line classes and distance learning. They also have a free e-newsletter and tons of other good stuff.

5

Key #2

Timing

So you see, imagination needs moodling—long, inefficient, happy
idling, dawdling and puttering.
—Brenda Ueland, *If You Want to Write*

Earlier is not better! Abraham Lincoln said that if you have four hours
to cut down a tree, spend three hours sharpening the blade. Likewise,
it's ultimately inefficient—and possibly harmful—to press children to
attempt intellectual activities for which they're not ready. It's like trying to cut down the tree with a dull blade. Instead of getting the tree
cut down sooner, you waste all four hours. Better to sharpen the blade
first, and then proceed.

If we could wave a magic wand and change American schools, we
would change this: the idea that earlier is better, that there is some
intrinsic value in children's learning things (1) *on cue* and (2) *early.*
(Note: What we refer to as timing is also called *readiness,* a concept
that falls in and out of favor in American public school policy. Right
now, it's mostly out of favor.) Our experience, and a large body of
research in developmental psychology, insists that there is enormous,
mostly unrecognized value in children simply being allowed to learn
things when they are *ready.*

Most people assume that babies have an innate timetable for new teeth, rolling over, acquiring language, and walking (although these areas, too, are contaminated with a widespread earlier-means-smarter anxiety). But we fail to consider that an innate timetable may also apply for reading, math, and other intellectual skills. In fact, our culture's puritanical bias may even suggest that learning is somehow more valuable when it occurs counter to a child's innate timetable.

Yet some research suggests exactly the reverse. For example, one study indicated that children introduced to formal reading instruction in second grade instead of first not only "caught up" by the fourth grade but became more enthusiastic, spontaneous readers in adolescence. Other studies suggest that children have natural timetables for cognitive development. Indeed, the human brain may be extremely specialized and compartmentalized in its intellectual functions, with different brain structures responsible for discerning various types of knowledge. These structures may mature at different rates in the same person—for instance, a child may be ahead of peers in reading, behind peers in understanding numbers, and in the middle in pattern recognition. These cognitive development timetables, which are thought to be genetically determined, often are violated by the earlier-is-better schedules of schools. Recent brain research may explain the costs of such violation: The child's brain adapts and uses "inappropriate" structures to accomplish the demanded tasks. When the preferred brain structures are "ready" to attempt the functions that they evolved to perform, they lack stimulation, and long-term learning difficulties can ensue.

The work of Jean Piaget (1896–1980), a Swiss psychologist who pioneered studies of children's intellectual development, continues to heavily influence psychologists and educators. Piaget described the stages each child's mind moves through in order to construct its internal representation of the world. He argued that normal children acquire the ability to understand *symbols* at around the age of seven and to understand *second-order* symbols (symbols *about* symbols) at around the age of twelve. Roughly put, that might mean a two-year-old can count, a seven-year-old can multiply, and a twelve-year-old can understand algebra. While Piaget's work has been questioned, modified, and challenged in myriad ways, his basic ideas are still widely accepted. Also widely accepted is the idea that these new skill levels emerge naturally from within the child's developing mind. It is odd, given that this philosophy is the closest thing to a consensus about childhood development that exists in educational theory, that many schools (often because of policies at higher government levels) ignore its principles and insist on introducing age-inappropriate material on the earlier-is-better theory.

Of course, some kids fall at the fast end of the timing continuum—at least in some areas. (One way Piaget's work currently is being modified is in the questioning of his assumption that a child's various intellectual capacities—reasoning, analytical, verbal, and so on—progress at about the same rate. More typically, a child may be "ahead" in one skill and "behind" in another.) Sensitivity to the needs of faster-developing kids might include making sure they have stimulating, challenging work to do in their areas of interest—in school if possible, out of school otherwise. Some inflexible teachers may insist that these kids do busywork far below their level of competence because the rest of the class is doing it. They'd be better off, in our view, sitting in a corner reading, drawing, working ahead in the textbook, or leaving class for tutoring by an older student. (We don't care for the common "gifted and talented" label and the practice of removing these kids from the "normal" class, partly because this label implies that the speed of development is somehow related to one's ultimate gifts or talents. It's not. We also don't like the stigma attached to the "nongifted" kids—the idea that the question is not *what* your gifts are, but whether you *have* any!—nor the fact that G&T programs are often the only places in schools where learning is vital and fun.)

In any event, whether your child is a "late" bloomer or an "early" bloomer, it's all a matter of paying careful, unprejudiced, flexible attention to your children, day by day, to discern what their needs may be at a given time, regardless of the category that their school assigns to them.

Too often, children are viewed as if they were lab rats, whose behavior can be managed and controlled through the application of reward and punishment, the aim being to teach them the fanciest tricks. In actuality, of course, children are human beings with human spirits, whose own wishes *matter*. Instead of worrying about which grade or class or school or level your child "should" be in, as if some objective expert witness could have the unimpeachable answer, try asking your child what she or he *wants*. There is no dishonor in parents' ensuring that their children have the best possible opportunities and the most challenging projects; the problem arises when we become so anxious that we try to force children to conform to expectations—our own or others'—that we leave out the most important part of the equation: the child's spirit.

ATTENDING TO THE SPIRIT (AND TIMING) OF YOUR CHILD

We hurry our children to learn, to grow, to attend lessons and activities, to go to school. Like the hurrying that we imagine will result in more knowledge, we hurry our children out of the nest and into institutions run by strangers whose interaction with them is not always informed by love. As a society it sometimes seems as if we believe that hurrying our children into regimentation will make them tough and realistic, keep them from being vulnerably dependent on the protection of loving parents. Yet like academic hurrying, this independence-hurrying often has an effect contrary to our intentions. Paradoxically, it may prevent kids from growing up strong and independent. Independence grows from unconditional love, trust, and having one's appropriate dependency needs met, not from premature withdrawal of support. Perhaps our pressure on our children to grow, to learn, and to achieve is a reflection of our own way of being, as we hurry ourselves from task to task, from job to home, and through each moment, absorbed in our thoughts and anxieties, reacting rather than responding, acting from fear rather than love. Allowing our children the freedom to develop their own interests, to respond authentically to opportunities, and to grow and learn at their own pace is nothing less than refusing to indulge our fears and anxieties about the future and instead taking a courageous stand on behalf of love.

The rhythm of the authentic, soul-based, inner-grounded life is slow and unworried. In it, we step outside of time, outside of the panicked cravings to achieve, to overcome, and to win, and outside of the desire to control ourselves and others. Here there is time for real learning. Here we can trust our children to grow and to learn at their own pace. Here we can refuse "the world" and attend to our souls. Here we can let go of an anxious, future-fearing mode of parenting that demands we sacrifice our children's present for some vaguely threatening future in which they and we will come up short. And here, sometimes ironically, our minds find fertile ground for new growth. After an acquaintance of Grace's decided to try home-schooling with his eleven-year-old son, he anxiously waited for the boy to take an interest in something and get moving—while his son apparently wanted nothing more than to stare out the window. Grace reassured him that most new homeschoolers need time just to "detox" and recuperate from the pressures of school. After a couple months elapsed, the man reported that his son had indeed continued to stare out the window. But it turned out that the boy had begun noticing birds out there. Soon he started looking those birds up in a field guide, and then he began sketching them and making notes. Most recently, he had signed up to participate in an Audubon Society field study, helping to count and identify the different birds in his area.

Why is it so difficult for us to respect our children's timing? Because we want so much for our children and for ourselves, and because we as adults are so often in a hurried panic about everything. Because rush is the air we breathe. Because we're fraught with worry that our kids will end up on the streets if they're the last in their class to learn their multiplication tables.

And because, although there's no inherent problem with kids learning things at different times, within the school system there are real consequences for being slow. Kids who learn things later than other kids can, in fact, be held back a grade, put in stigmatized groups or classes for "slow" kids, be subject to teachers' and kids' disrespect, and feel confused and lost when a class is learning a skill that builds on another skill with which they're not yet comfortable. These are very real problems, but the way to address them is *not* to hurry your child; rather, do what you can to change the situation, reassure your child that there's nothing wrong with him, tell him (truthfully) that you'll work together to make sure that he need suffer no long-term consequences for marching to his own beat, and help him—when he is

Randi Lewis: "Our son William has just turned five and is in a pre-K program, a very intentional, loving, nurturing place. The parents are all pushing the teachers (who very much believe in the importance of play) to give their preschoolers homework! They say their kids want to do more academic stuff! I disagree with this approach wholeheartedly. People keep coming to me and saying, 'Aren't you concerned? Is William reading yet? Is he adding?'

"Well, William actually is adding—because he wants to! He's got fingers, and they're cool! Major excitement! But if we are cramming learning down our kids' throats because we are uptight about it and it's something we need them to do, it's detrimental. It doesn't work. Developmentally, kids read when they are ready to read. I believe that wholeheartedly. My daughter, Sydney, started reading when she was four—she's just very visual! Back then, everybody kept coming up to me and saying 'Which program are you using?' We're not using a 'program'! We *read*! All the time! And we talk all the time! William's not reading, and he's nowhere ready to read. He'll read when he's ready.

"William loves to be read to. He's certainly just as enthusiastic about literature as my daughter was. We do a lot of dictating stories. Now my son will dictate stories to my daughter, which is a beautiful thing to see. Or he'll say to me, '*Robin!* Do I hear a *B* in there?' It's happening not because we're sitting down with flash cards, just because it's an opportunity and he can't wait! It's a totally natural thing. I know there are some kids that it doesn't come naturally to, but I do believe that it's generally a natural skill."

ready to and wants your help—to learn the skills he is "behind" in. This practical approach is a far cry from trying to fix, rush, accelerate your kids, or catch them up. Whenever you hear them or you or anyone say your children are "behind," STOP! "Behind" is an imaginary and basically useless concept.

Respecting our children's timing means not only allowing them to start learning a subject when they're ready to but also respecting their pace once they do begin. Some children will start to learn something early but learn it slowly overall, some will delay beginning but pick it

Nathen Lester, a twenty-eight-year-old recording engineer and musician from Southern California, shared this story: "I was about nine when I expressed an interest in playing the mandolin to my dad. I can now imagine how excited he was at this since he is a musician and this was the first sign I had shown that I might follow in his footsteps. Within a few days he had rented a mandolin and showed me a few chords. He put it in my room, laying open in its case. I never touched it. I never even thought about playing it. I was busy reading and playing in the woods. After a couple weeks I noticed that it was gone. My dad never rebuked me or even mentioned it. That's so impressive to me now that he knew me and trusted me so much that he could let it go like that, and that it didn't affect his support of my musical interests in the future. Now I am a musician. I wonder how my life would be different if he had manipulated me somehow into playing the mandolin before I chose to pick it up on my own."

up quickly once they do start, some begin early and move along in a snap, and others will delay beginning and learn slowly. *It's all okay.*

We've all noticed how children learn things in bursts—they may do nothing for a long time and then all at once make big strides. And if we pay attention to our adult selves, most of us will notice that we, too, learn and do things in uneven increments. We forget this when our kids go through a period of apparent dormancy or downtime, particularly at school or in an academic area; we'd do them a great service by keeping it in mind.

FACE YOUR OWN FEARS ABOUT "LATE" BLOOMERS

At the most basic level, in order to begin respecting our kids' natural rhythms, we have to face our *own* anxiety. We worry that there's a magical age by which if you haven't done certain things, you lose. If you haven't learned a second language by age five, it's too late to become fluent. If you haven't learned to read by the end of second grade, you'll always be a slow student. If you get behind in math, you'll miss important "building blocks" and never catch up. If you haven't learned to make a Web page by now, you never will. As a society, we increasingly take fears like these to extremes, applying them to kindergartners and even preschoolers.

Even when we intellectually know better and refrain from overt pushing, kids intuit our feelings just as clearly as they hear our out-loud nagging. It can help to do some inner work on ourselves, to stop and deal with our fears, one by one. (Of course, once you name them, they might immediately sound less convincing than when you just carry their weight around unconsciously—and that's part of our purpose.)

Try this: Choose something you're worried about your child not being up-to-speed in—reading, arithmetic skills, physical coordination, social skills, career plans, whatever. Now carry your fear to its logical conclusion, by inquiring into it and asking yourself questions like these: How likely is it that _____? What's the worst that can happen if _____? Now, is that a likely or necessary outcome if _____? Would that really be a problem, if that did happen? What would that mean; *how* exactly would it be a problem? How could we avoid it happening, or mitigate its damage, *besides* pushing and hurrying our child along? All right, given all of that, do I need to worry?

Your internal dialogue might go something like this:

Right now it's February, and Rosie is one of three kids in her first-grade class who really can't read—she knows the sounds individual letters make and has memorized some books so that she can pretend to read, but she just doesn't read words yet. And I'm worried that she won't by the end of first grade. Okay, I'm going to take a deep breath and really look at this. First, how likely is it that Rosie really won't be able to read by the end of this year? Well, the truth is that I don't know what's going to happen, and nobody else does either. She could go either way. Is there anything I can do besides pushing her to help her learn to read faster? Well, not really. I already read to her every night and talk with her about words and letters, and I've asked her if she wants extra help learning to read and she said "no."

All right then, what's the worst possible scenario here? What's the worst that can happen if she doesn't learn to read by the end of first grade? Well, she could be held back a year. Wow, my face is getting hot, and I can feel my belly clenching. I remember how when I went to school, we made fun of the kids who flunked a grade. And I'm already thinking about what my mother-in-law would say. I guess I'm worried about the social stigma—both for Rosie and, it looks like, for me too. That's the answer to the next question: what would be the worst thing that would happen if she were held back? Both the social stigma—what other people thought of us—and also Rosie's own self-esteem: I don't want her to think of herself as a failure, especially not at such a young, vulnerable age. And then there's also just the sense of wasted time—would she really benefit from spending an extra year in school?

Okay, so now I'm going to look more closely at these issues: social stigma, self-esteem, and wasted time. If Rosie were held back for a year, are these inevitable results? Well, the social stigma—that's not something we can do a whole lot to control. Other kids might tease her; it's even possible that some of her future teachers might see her as inferior for that reason. Self-esteem, on the other hand; that's definitely in our control—well, ultimately it's in Rosie's control, but I can have a lot to do with it. I'm sure there are all kinds of ways we can address that. At some point in her life, if not now, Rosie will "fail" at something, and true self-esteem will survive failure, might even grow out of failure. That'll be a tough one, but we can handle it.

As for the wasted time . . . I don't know. Maybe if she stayed back a year now she might still be able to skip a grade later—if she felt ready to. Some kids graduate early these days, even when they don't skip grades; they just plan their credits thoughtfully. If that became important to her, we could help her plan for that. It's more of a long shot, but she could also apply for early admission to a college. Or, to look at it from the opposite direction, another possibility would be to just take her out of school for the rest of this year and let her join that home-school co-op playgroup I read about in the paper. Then she could go into first grade the following fall. Hmmmm. . . . That might take more effort on my part than I'm ready to give. But let me find out more about it before I decide against it.

As you start to make your vague fears concrete, the fear-based, anxious workings of your mind may begin to seem less convincing. And as you can see from our example, one of the main benefits of thinking like this is that it helps you get out of worry and paralysis and into possibility. Even if Rosie ends up repeating the first grade and then simply proceeding through second through twelfth grades year by year, she will surely benefit from her parents' more open mental mindset—it's wider now, more helpful, a source of strength rather than of fear.

Susan Gushue (who, again, is a math tutor as well as the mother of five children): "You can start teaching them multiplication facts in first grade or in fourth grade. Unless there's something weird going on, at the end of fourth grade they'll know them."

Another way to start taking your fears less seriously is to talk about them openly with other people. Say to your friends "What do you think would happen if . . . ?" And seek out stories that contradict your fears—look for examples of kids who grew up okay even though they read late and the like. A superb source is *Growing Without Schooling* magazine (see "Timing Resources"), which frequently prints stories about late readers (although not nearly as many as it printed in the 1970s and 1980s, because now it's much more taken for granted in the homeschooling movement that reading late does not need to cause a problem). Read *An A in Life: Famous Homeschoolers*, by Mac and Nancy Plent (see "Timing Resources"), which tells about all kinds of successful people who were educational misfits in one way or another. For that matter, just read lots of autobiographies in general, and you'll encounter the same theme often. If you have a late bloomer on your hands, finding models of successful, happy late bloomers will reassure both you and your child.

If you recognize that it's important to you to allow your child to blossom at a natural rate, make sure you speak to his or her teacher about it. Some teachers automatically assume that parents are afraid their child will fall behind. Teachers can be anxious about a child's progress as a result of imagining *you're* anxious about it! If you think what your son needs is *less* pressure to read, tell his teacher that and discuss strategies for working together.

Also keep in mind that many of our fears are based on unexamined, murky assumptions—the results of TV commercials, our own parents' (unexamined) fears, platitudes we heard from our first-grade teachers, and the like. Regardless of the way society—or reality—actually is, we sometimes make our own reality much worse by thinking that people hate, judge, or have power over us more than they actually do. In other words, when we *imagine* we're controlled, we might as well actually *be* controlled—we'll put all the same limits on ourselves that our imagined oppressors would. The beauty is that when we can step out of this mental trap, there's not much around us that physically limits us in twenty-first-century America.

Sometimes, too, we're prey to an overarching, dark fear that perhaps the timing will *never* arrive for some things—will your son *never* tire of video games and take an interest in good books? Will your

---

Omar Collins: "Our oldest son, Fahiym, was in pre-K in a New York City school. He could already read and write when he showed up. It seemed like such a waste of his day to be sitting there learning colors. They were holding him back. 'We don't promote kids early,' we were told by the teacher and the principal. Then we found out they promoted another kid who was white. At that time, our family situation made it possible for my wife to stay home with the kids, so we took them out of school.

"At first, we started imitating 'school at home.' Certain strict times, certain subjects, my wife sitting down with them at the kitchen table. Then we got turned on to John Holt's books. His ideas were really right where we wanted to be. We stopped doing 'school at home' and just started homeschooling. We let the kids follow their interests. Homeschooling makes you take a look at yourself. Kids will pull you out of your comfort zone and make you stretch! It made my family closer than we would have been.

"My daughter loved to read—she was complaining all the time at school that she could only check one book out at a time. After we took her out of school, she'd go to the library and get twenty books out."

daughter *never* feel ready to learn fractions? Again, it helps to put these ghosts in perspective—first, by asking yourself how realistic your fears are, and, second, by taking an objective view: What if your daughter finds herself at the age of eighty, lying on her deathbed, without knowing how to work with fractions? Will that be the end of the world? Is that possibility worth your anxiety and fear *now*?

Supporting Early Bloomers

> When I was about thirteen, the library was going to get *Calculus for the Practical Man*. By this time I knew, from reading the encyclopedia, that calculus was an important and interesting subject, and I ought to learn it. When I finally saw the calculus book at the library, I was very excited. I went to the librarian to check it out, but she looked at me and said, 'You're just a child. What are you taking this book out for?' It was one of the few times in my life I was uncomfortable and I lied. I said it was for my father.
>
> —Richard Feynman[1]

As we said earlier, honoring your children's natural timing also, of course, means: Don't hold them back. Some children need relatively large amounts of stimulation, challenge, and even competition to be fully engaged, vital, and learning. If your attentive observation of your child has led you to the insight that he or she is not getting enough interesting stimulation in school, you can try to change the situation there (again, you may meet resistance from overburdened or unsympathetic authorities) or you can try to supplement the school curriculum on your own.

If your kids are shy or well behaved, keep your eyes open for ways they restrain themselves in order not to offend others, draw attention

---

[1] Richard Feynman, *Surely You're Joking, Mr. Feynman! Adventures of a Curious Character* (New York: Norton, 1997).

Celia Waddell, of Olga, Missouri, writes: "My daughter Clare, who is now six, surprised me when she was three by becoming interested in the American Girls Book series. This is a series of thirty-six historical fiction books for third- and fourth-grade readers. I was a little reluctant to read them to her at first. Soon, though, she convinced me. In the past three years I have read them all to her multiple times and she has a very good grasp of American history.

"Let me give you an example of one of the issues in the books. Addy, one of the six main characters, is a slave at the time of the Civil War. Her brother and father are sold from their plantation, and she and her mother decide they have to run away. They leave behind her baby sister.

"These are very intense issues, and the books convey a lot of fear. The family is separated for a long time. Clare just loves them. She asks questions that are hard to answer. Why did we have slavery, anyway? and Was the Civil War fought to free the slaves? are examples.

"Looking back, I am really glad that I agreed to this project. She was ready, especially if that means excited and interested, and she still is. Now she is in first grade, and an excellent reader."

 At the heart of Timing is: SENSITIVITY. Be sensitive to your child's ongoing developmental needs and capabilities. Work to create outer situations in harmony with the child's inner rhythms.

to themselves, or make waves. When Grace took piano lessons as a young child, she'd often peek ahead in her lesson books and learn to play much more difficult songs than she was currently assigned—yet, ironically, she felt guilty about this. In fact, she pretended to find these new pieces difficult when her teacher later introduced her to them. (Her parents didn't keep close enough tabs on her to realize what was going on, which was basically what she wanted—she liked the independence of being responsible for her own practice.) There was no real harm done, but it would have been nice if someone would have realized that Grace was moving ahead and said "Good for you!"

TIMING STRATEGIES—FOR LATE BLOOMERS, EARLY BLOOMERS, AND THOSE BLOOMERS CONSIDERED ON TRACK

- Pay attention. If a young child seems fatigued and exhausted by the ready-to-read flash cards you're introducing, *stop*. If your seven-year-old is extremely frustrated by her reading assignments, consider arranging to have them reduced. A child who finds algebra mystifying and complex one year may find it a cinch the next. Your sensitive attention also may reveal a child who is bored or frustrated by a too-slow pace in class.
- Don't try to "teach" your kids too often. Discuss enthusiastically what you're interested in and what they're interested in, but pay attention to when you're losing them. Less is more. Nobody wants to be preached to. Listen. Wait for them to ask questions, and then err on the side of underanswering.
- Affirm to your kids that there's no hurry by speaking to them in "patient talk." Whether you're talking about academia, dating, choosing a career, or even (if you can do so honestly) cleaning their room, frequently use phrases and sentences like "whenever you're ready," "no rush," "I'm not in a hurry," "you don't need to hurry." Although kids' lives may look easy to adults, children themselves can feel tremendous pressure. Remember your own childhood, your burdens of worries about homework, social situations, or things you desperately wanted and felt you would never have. Talking like this can calm them greatly and allay their fears.
- Understand that different interests or projects have different natural life cycles. Some are long, some ephemeral. Longer isn't always better. And don't be too seduced by kids' own expectations for themselves. Say your son has set a goal for himself of writing a novel, but he's quit partway through and is disap-

Timing Exercises

For you:

Look into your past and write down three academic subjects or skills you felt pushed or rushed to learn. Choose one (as simple as memorizing multiplication tables or as complex as calculus) that you still feel a bit traumatized about but that you imagine could benefit your life now. Ask yourself: Am I ready to learn it now? If so, start out as an absolute beginner, and make it yours. You could learn on your own (with flash cards, textbooks, Web sites, CD-ROMs, books, videos, experiments, or observation) or with flesh-and-blood help (a study circle, college class, mentor, tutor, kindly neighbor, teenage daughter). Above all, *don't rush.* Take your time and savor your new skills and understanding. Notice how your pace slows and speeds up at different junctures along the way.

For your kids:

Name a fear you hold about your child's progress or development, and proceed through a series of what's-the-worst-that-will-happen questions (as we did earlier in the chapter), until you arrive at your ultimate worry. Then do some follow-up research to challenge your fears. Be gentle with yourself. Also ask: Where did I get these ideas in the first place?

Randi Lewis: "My daughter will be 'ahead' in life not because she read at age four but for other reasons. She has been communicated with so much that she knows how to ask for what she needs to know. I don't think that being 'ahead' is the thing that's going to make her successful, by any means. The speed of it doesn't offer them anything."

---

pointed in himself. You can bring a helpful perspective to the situation by saying "Good for you—you got interested in writing and explored it seriously for a while. Now you're ready to do something else instead. No problem." Help children see what they learned from each project, whether it matched their expectations or not.

- Don't rush your kids into independence. Many public kindergartens have switched from half-day to full-day programs, not for the benefit of the children but for the convenience of working parents. Yet in our experience, many teachers and principals convey to parents the impression that there is something wrong with a child who doesn't want to go to kindergarten all day at the age of five, or with a parent who is concerned about the child's well-being in those circumstances. We're not saying there's necessarily anything wrong with sending children to full-day kindergarten; we're suggesting that there's nothing wrong with *not* sending them either. Parents who are calmly confident that their children will develop the appropriate skills, competencies, and independence when they're ready, without worrying too much about whether they're ahead of or behind their peers, tend to raise competent, independent kids.
- Intervene on your children's behalf at school if they seem stressed out. You might request alternative or shorter assignments, or attempt to change the class or track your kids are in.
- Above all, keep the whole person in mind. What kind of adult would you like to see your child grow into? In this context, the meaning of a particular task or skill might shift.

Resources

Elkind, David. *The Hurried Child.* New York: Alfred A. Knopf, 1984.

Growing Without Schooling (GWS) magazine. Holt Associates, 2380 Mass. Avenue, Suite 104, Cambridge, MA 02140. The original homeschooling magazine, founded by John Holt, contains hundreds of stories about kids who were allowed to read, learn math, or do various other academic things "late" and who caught up when they were ready.

Healy, Jane. *Endangered Minds: Why Our Children Can't Think and What We Can Do about It.* New York: Simon and Schuster, 1990.

Holt, John. *Escape From Childhood: The Needs and Rights of Children.* New York: Holt Associates, 1996.

Kraus, Robert. *Leo the Late Bloomer.* New York: HarperCollins Juvenile, 1998.

Luvmour, Sambhava, and Josette Luvmour. *Natural Learning Rhythms: How and When Children Learn.* Berkeley, CA: Celestial Arts, 1993.

Plent, Mac and Nancy. *An A in Life: Famous Homeschoolers.* Available from John Holt's Bookstore (www.holtgws.com).

Singer, Dorothy G., and Tracey Revenson. *A Piaget Primer: How a Child Thinks.* New York: Plume, 1996.

6
Key #3

Interest

One never learns to understand truly anything but what one loves.
—Johan Wolfgang von Goethe, *18th century German poet*

Interest is the magic ingredient, the pixie dust of Guerrilla Learning. In a pinch, most kids can manage to learn (albeit in a hobbled fashion) without proper attention to the other keys—opportunity, timing, freedom, and support. But they don't learn—not really—without being interested. You can lead a horse to water, but you can't make her drink.

Recognize this truth for yourself. Take a moment and remember a time when you had to learn something that you were not in the least interested in—at school, at church, or at work, or in some other context. Recall what studying felt like, consider whether you remember the material now, and notice the feelings you still have associated with the subject. (Amy still remembers begging her boss to let her out of a dreadful class in the C programming language that was required for all computer programmers on staff at her job, even though her job would never oblige her to use that language.) Now think of a time when you pursued something you *were* interested in—whether you took it up on your own or were inspired by a teacher or someone else. Recall the experience of learning that material. How do you feel about the subject now? How much of it do you recall?

You may not find a complete and direct cause-and-effect relationship between interest and learning, but we bet you'll find at least a strong correlation. Generally, when we learn due to interest, it's pleasurable, straightforward, and effective. When we learn due to coercion, it's unpleasant, difficult, and useless—and we often forget the learned material as soon as we can afford to.

It turns out there may be a biological basis for this: Joseph Chilton Pearce, whose books on childhood development (including *Magical Child*, cited in "Interest Resources") have profoundly influenced many parents, differentiates between true learning and "conditioning." According to recent research, he says, conditioning is a fear-based response grounded in the survival-oriented "reptilian" brain, while true learning takes place in the frontal lobes. Conditioned learning is associated with hostile or anxious emotional states. At the first sign of anxiety, the brain shifts its functions to the reptilian brain, and true learning stops.[1]

Interest can be inspired, but it can't be *forced*. Much of school life revolves around how to teach, or learn, material that a child has no interest in or is not ready for. Many teachers view their jobs, and admirably so, as a process of trying to *get* children interested in material so that the power of interest-led learning will kick in. This works with some kids some of the time, of course, but not with all kids all of the time, even for extraordinary teachers.

INTEREST AND CHARACTER

I am the genius of myself.
—James P. Carse, *Finite and Infinite Games*

As Thomas Armstrong says in his book, *Awakening Your Child's Natural Genius* (see "Interest Resources"), every child is a genius in the original sense of the word: to be born or come into being. "In ancient

---

[1] Chris Mercogliano and Kim Debus, "An Interview with Joseph Chilton Pearce," in *Journal of Family Life*, vol. 5, No. 1, 1999, p. 21.

times, all persons were believed to possess a personal genius or attendant spirit that was given to them at birth and that governed their fortunes in life and determined their essential character. In the same way, your child has a light that shines brightly from deep within and represents her own inner wisdom," writes Armstrong.[2]

A child's emerging interests are the signs that can reveal his unique calling. Children don't know where their interests will lead them; neither do their parents. Yet these interests are not arbitrary or capricious. They are intrinsically related to a child's special, irreplaceable vision and gifts. Amy once heard author Deepak Chopra say that a parent's role is to help kids find out what they're meant to do. Honoring their interests may be one of the most important ways to do that.

None of us knows what our children's calling will be—indeed, many of us don't know what our own is! Hence we don't know how our child's calling is related to academic success. While school aims to expose children to as wide an unspecialized spectrum of learning and information as possible, the opportunity to pursue one's true interests in depth—and therefore truly learn something—often suffers from this "shotgun" approach. To the extent that school occupies much of children's time with meaningless busywork, and constantly ranks and criticizes their performance, academic success actually may displace their natural ability to explore and discover their true calling. The job of the Guerrilla Learning parent is to reverse the damage by noticing, honoring, and encouraging a child's developing interests.

> Pablo Picasso resisted school stubbornly and seemed completely unable to learn to read or write. The other students grew used to seeing him come late with his pet pigeon—and with the paintbrush he always carried as if it were an extension of his own body.
> —Authors Mildred and Victor Goertzel, *300 Eminent Personalities*

Part of honoring a child's unique character and interests is allowing the space for your child to be different from *you*. An introverted child

---

[2] Thomas Armstrong, Ph.D., *Awakening Your Child's Natural Genius* (New York: Tarcher, 1991), p. 3.

in an extroverted family, a sports lover in a family of bookworms, or a musician in a family of natural athletes may find her interests belittled, ignored, or manipulated. In subtler ways, when children have different interests, learning styles, or social styles from their parents or siblings, parents may have to make an effort to honor and understand these children. One child is drawn to solitary pursuits, another to team sports, a third to endless conversation with friends. Rather than attempting to correct any of these tendencies, Guerrilla Learning parents would recognize emerging gifts for solitude and introspection, for leadership and organization, or for the kind of personal intimacy that makes one a good therapist, respectively. And while we can all benefit from developing our weaknesses as well as our strengths, a Guerrilla Learning parent is in no hurry to push a child into an uncomfortable direction, unless the child has asked for such help.

> When your imagination awakens, then you begin to realize that one of
> the great loyalties in life is faithfulness to your own originality. And
> that anything that contains you, or limits you, or is too small for that
> originality is too small for the great force and sacrament of your life.
> —John O'Donohue, *The Divine Imagination*

Our approach to interest is *not* about how to "get" kids interested in things. In our view, parents do that best by providing kids with lots of rich, stimulating, exciting opportunities in which to participate (as we discussed in Chapter 4, "Opportunity"). What they choose to be interested in is ultimately and entirely up to them. Besides, if your children are attending school, they probably are already being exposed to a number of subject areas in which they may not have a natural interest.

Nor are we concerned with how to "use" kids' interests to "get" them to learn specific information. Guerrilla Learning is about providing kids with the space and support they need to pursue what *they're* interested in. To some extent, we can work within the schools

At the heart of Interest is: INDIVIDUALITY. Help your children identify their unique talents, gifts, and passions. Honor their originality. Their job is to develop their inner natures and to find their calling in life.

to use them as resources to accommodate our kids' interests. To some extent, we can help our kids make it through the parts of school that bore, frustrate, or even upset them. Otherwise, we can provide as much freedom and support as our resources allow to help children explore their interests in what's left of their lives after school is over.

INTEREST STRATEGIES

- The best thing you can do for your children is simple but harder than it sounds: *Commit yourself to the faith that your kids are here to grow into the best possible versions of themselves*—not to become what you or anyone else thinks they should become. And back off. Whereas it's up to you to surround your kids with opportunity and respect their timing, it's up to your kids to actually *be* interested. It's their job, not yours. Yours is to chill out, recognize their interests, come to terms with your own feelings and judgments about those interests, and ultimately honor each child's unique nature.
- *Recognize your kids.* Pay attention to them. Acknowledge them. Know them better than they know themselves. It feels deep-down good to be really seen by people we love and who love us. That's a world away, of course, from how it feels when someone who doesn't really love or respect us spies on us, watches us in order to figure out our weaknesses, and then preys on them or tries to fix them. Sometimes when we pay attention to our older children, they seem to want to shut us out at times. But more often than not their defensive gestures are a sham, a test: *Do you really*

love me enough to stay interested in me, even when I'm a snotty brat? Is your love unconditional? Older kids very much want their parents' attention; they want to be known. That desire may co-exist (and seem to conflict) with their being embarrassed by you in the presence of their peers, with anger, with their desire for autonomy. But it's pervasive and strong—and you recognize that in your own life, right? You want your own parents to know you deeply and to accept and love you for exactly who you are even now, as an adult.

- Find out about your kids' passions, interests, and goals, and honor them. Even—especially—if they're things you disapprove of. Amy remembers a long dinner conversation about the *Star Wars* film series that specifically addressed the question posed by Elijah: Who is the most powerful Jedi in all the *Star Wars* movies? The discussion eventually revolved around the idea of power vs. strength. Carsie pointed out that Darth Vader became more powerful than the emperor when he realized he loved his son because love allowed the Force to work through him more fully. Amy felt that Yoda was the most powerful, even though we never see him fight or control others, because he wisely guides others in developing and using their power. "My theory is that Darth Vader is the most powerful," concluded Elijah, "because he killed the emperor, who was the most powerful up until then." (Okay, he was six.) We use this example in part because we have heard many adults criticizing the *Star Wars* series because of violence or commercialism; perhaps they have failed to recognize the mythic resonance of the story and the great power it holds to capture kids' imaginations by dramatizing the very issues and feelings that confront them as they grow. Kids don't choose their interests for no reason, and parents sometimes just need to drop their critical distance and put themselves in their kids' world.

- Distinguish your own feelings from what you think your kids need. To some degree and in some cases, you *can* "get" your kids interested in things, and that's all well and good, and why we wrote Chapter 4, "Opportunity." In this way you offer your child a chance to discover something new that intrigues him or her.

But you and your kids will reap a different kind of benefit, just as valuable, from your working on *yourself*—your recognizing that *what* they're interested in may not be as important as you think it is, as long as they're interested in *something*, and that to a large degree you can't change their interests anyway.

- Examine your biases toward your kids' different interests. Many times teenagers especially acquire interests their parents really hate—rock music, witchcraft, anarchy. Or, in these changing times, sometimes Nazi-style militarism or religious fundamentalism. Ironically, when parents don't make a big deal about hating their kids' "hateful" interests, those subjects can lose their significance and much of their appeal. Now, sex and drugs and rock and roll *are* interesting; it's easy to see why kids (and adults) get fascinated by them. But when kids aren't pursuing them out of rebellion, they're less energetic and confused about them. They're in a better position to sort out *for themselves* what they want, what's best for them given the whole picture of their lives.

- Sometimes you might choose to help a child pursue an interest even if it means keeping him or her out of school. Doing so helps to send the message that school is part of the larger context of learning, not vice versa; that you care more about your kids' learning than their schoolwork. (And, of course, it can provide great delight for children, fostering a feeling that school doesn't "own" them. You may want not to go out of your way to emphasize that, but there's no harm in letting them relish the feeling.) Amy's family travels a lot, and when Carsie has been in school her teachers were always supportive of her missing school for a trip. Sometimes Carsie kept a photojournal of her trip, sometimes she researched the local culture or government, and sometimes she just brought back an interesting local artifact or craft to share with her teachers and class.

- Be sensitive to the possibility that a child may want to keep her hobby or interest all to herself. But don't automatically keep your distance out of an assumption that she wants you to do so. Check it out; find out how she really feels—and then keep checking from time to time, because those feelings may change.

Interest Exercises

For you:

1. Uncover an undeveloped interest in your own life by making a list of abandoned childhood passions or playing detective: Consider your taste in TV/movies, what kinds of stores you window-shop in, topics you get excited about talking about with your friends. It can be something "academic" like Civil War history or geology or the Italian language, or something "banal" like fashion, fast cars, how to make decadent delicious desserts, or the personal lives of your favorite movie stars. Pursue your interest if you wish, to whatever degree you wish.

2. If you're not in the habit already, choose one of your interests and practice sharing your excitement about it with your children—not to teach them something or get them to "be" some way, but to feel the unique thrill of enthusiastically communicating to someone else your own joy. (Of course, don't overdo it. You don't want them to groan every time you bring up the subject of delta blues guitar or Shaker furniture.)

For your kids:

1. Be a detective in terms of your kids' interests—what comes out in the hidden cracks of life? What comes out in conversation? How does your son decorate his room, what stores does he like, what TV shows and movies appeal to him, how does he dress? Of course, a lot of this (especially if he's a teenager) may simply reveal his chosen identity of the month, the group whose approval he craves. That, too, provides clues as to his nature and interests, but it's also helpful to sort out what comes more independently and uniquely from within. What does your kid do or like that his friends don't do or like also?

2. Practice being interested in your child's interests. When your child shares something she's interested in—even if it's something "unimportant," like a new Lego model or a TV show—ask open-ended questions. Listen. Be enthusiastic. Pay attention especially to interests you don't approve of. If your teenage daughter is thrilled by a rock band that makes you cringe, ask her what she likes about the band. Ask her to play you her favorite song. You don't have to pretend you like it—but you just may be surprised by what you hear.

Resources

Armstrong, Thomas. *Awakening Your Child's Natural Genius: Enhancing Curiosity, Creativity, and Learning Ability.* New York: Tarcher/Putnam, 1991.

Holt, John. *Learning All the Time.* Reading, MA: Perseus, 1989.

Kohl, Herbert. *The Question Is College: On Finding and Doing Work You Love.* Portsmouth, NH: Heinemann, 1989.

Pearce, Joseph Chilton. *Magical Child.* New York: Plume, 1977, 1992.

Sher, Barbara. *I Could Do Anything If I Only Knew What it Was: How to Discover What You Really Want and How to Get It.* New York: Dell, 1995.

———. *Wishcraft: How to Get What You Really Want.* New York: Ballantine, 1979.

7
Key #4
Freedom

Each weekday while my father worked on his Sunday sermon, I attended the school of the Reverend Maclean. He taught nothing but reading and writing, and, being a Scot, believed that the art of writing lay in thrift. So while my friends spent their days at Missoula Elementary, I stayed home and learned to write the American language. However, there was a balance to my father's system. Every afternoon I was set free, untutored and untouched 'til supper, to learn on my own the natural side of God's order.

—Norman Maclean, *A River Runs through It*

FREEDOM MEANS CHOICE

We tag "freedom" with all kinds of clichéd romantic images: long hair lifting in the breeze, horses galloping through the sunrise surf, eagles floating over canyons. No plans, no worries, nothing heavy. To be sure, all of us, young and old, need that kind of no-responsibility refuge from time to time. But freedom-as-refuge isn't what we want to talk about here. Freedom is not the same as mere liberty to follow our desires and impulses. The person who automatically follows every impulse is not free at all but is a slave of desire. Freedom, as some philosophers have described it, is essentially the freedom to commit oneself, and that's what interests us: *the freedom to choose and to commit.* We'll talk here about the freedom *to* do and be what we can, more so than the freedom *from* rules and limits.

If an adult chooses to learn a foreign language, he makes a commitment to attend a class, to pay, and to study. He can't just do anything he feels like to learn the language; or, at least, not without either changing his mind or compromising his integrity. On the contrary: The freedom to commit oneself comes with certain obligations. If a child chooses to take piano lessons, her choice might mean a certain amount of practice and a commitment to stick with it for a certain number of weeks or months. A Guerrilla Learning parent acts as what Dr. Thomas Armstrong[1] calls a "choice coach"—helping a child to understand what the possibilities are and what the consequences of each choice may be.

As adults, we have fundamental choices about how to live our lives: what kind of work to do, whether to live alone or with someone, how many children to have, what interests and hobbies to pursue. Each choice carries with it a set of requirements and obligations. And so we spend a certain amount of time each day fulfilling those obligations: earning a living, caring for our families, doing chores, paying bills, even shopping for supplies for the stained-glass class we enthusiastically registered for.

Children also spend a portion of their days fulfilling obligations, from brushing their teeth to doing homework. As passionate advocates of giving children the maximum amount of freedom possible, we want to make it clear that *freedom is not inconsistent with obligation.* Rather, freedom means *choice.* Some things we have practically no choice about—we have to pay the bills, unless we want to live on the street, and our kids have to brush their teeth. Children benefit from being clearly told when they have a choice and when they don't rather than from some pretense that they *always* have a choice, or a broader range of choices than they actually do have.

Also, in advocating freedom for our children, we don't advocate a lack of discipline or guidance. As adults, we have experience and knowledge of the world that our children don't have. That experience and knowledge prepare us to lovingly guide our children in

---

[1] Dr. Armstrong is an influential educator and psychologist whose nine books include *The Myth of the A.D.D. Child, Awakening Your Child's Natural Genius,* and *Multiple Intelligences in the Classroom.*

ways that protect them while allowing them to exercise their growing competencies and powers. However, discipline is *not* the same thing as control, manipulation, coercion, or punishment. Parents overcontrol when they are afraid of their children's autonomy, when they are angry—often at people or circumstances they *can't* control—or when they haven't taken the time or energy to think a situation through and develop limits appropriate to the child's needs. Much parenting advice consists of tips on how better to manipulate and control children into compliance. In our view, a more healthy and effective form of parenting is to provide unconditional love and support within wide but steadfast limits. Children want and need parents to be powerful and strong and to enforce the limits they set. However, they don't want or need parents to control each aspect of their lives or interfere continuously with their autonomy. We believe that when parents practice providing more and more freedom to their children—without removing loving limits to behavior—they'll be surprised by children's ability to commit themselves and to follow through without control. (As we'll discuss in Chapter 8, "Support," they may also be surprised by how much support the children want, need, and request once they have become passionate about their goals.)

The power in giving children the maximum amount of freedom possible is that then they can take responsibility for their choices. We have seen countless cases of parents who decided a child should take music lessons, then impotently tried to force or coerce or wheedle or overpower the child into practicing. Yet parents who offer the child an authentic choice at the outset can step out of the teacher-child relationship and make themselves available for support when requested. The child might only need to be reminded, occasionally, that she made the choice to study piano and that she was aware of the requirements at the time. The consequences of failing to keep one's promises—disappointing the teacher, wasting money—can also be made clear. The parent no longer needs to "make" the child do anything. At the worst, the child can benefit from discovering what it feels like when we fail to accomplish goals that we ourselves set. In this chapter, we'll present ways for you to approach your children's learning in this way.

MANAGING OUR FEARS

Some parents want intuitively to provide more freedom, but fear doing their children a disservice. If we don't teach our children discipline, they worry, will they be effective adults? If we don't hold them to high standards and expectations, will they reach their potential? Aren't permissiveness and soft-heartedness to blame for the current breakdown of social structures, low student achievement, and moral relativism that sell our children short?

We don't trust these questions. The presumption that lies at their heart is: *People will be good only if they are forced to be.* The fundamental question, more honestly posed, would be: Are you going to force your children to be good or let them be bad? The dichotomy is false because, in fact, *people cannot be forced to be good.* Goodness counts only when it is freely chosen, as the biblical parable of the prodigal son illustrates. As stated in Luke 15:10, there is more "rejoicing in heaven" when a sinner like the prodigal younger son returns to God than when someone (like the older son) has spent his whole life dutifully going through the motions of obedience.

Distracted by the chaos and frenetic activity of our lives, we rob our kids—and ourselves—of the peace and solitude required for human beings to discover their inner guidance systems. Part of a healthy human being's inner guidance system is a love of learning, a wish to accomplish and to contribute to one's community, and a desire to be like the role models one respects. These are the kinds of "goodness" we want for our children—and which, alas, we anxiously attempt to instill in them by force. In trying to do more and more of what doesn't work, many of us fail to notice that these efforts are self-defeating.

THE POWER OF FREEDOM

Instead of trying to force them to be the way we think they *should* be, we can help our children grow by giving them lots of room, lots of choice. In the realm of education and learning, children—like adults—learn best when they have chosen to learn (as we discussed in

Chapter 6, "Interest"). While parents often want kids to earn their free-dom by proving that they're responsible, the flip side of that idea is that, generally speaking, giving freedom *helps* kids become responsible; withholding it keeps them dependent and passive. As we grant our chil-dren the freedom to make choices, they discover their inner guidance systems and begin to take responsibility for their own choices.

In other words, the purpose of giving our kids freedom is twofold. First, it allows them to fully develop their particular interests, and thus to enjoy their lives and their minds—right here, right now. And second, it helps them to develop their inner guidance systems, which will serve and direct them for the rest of their lives.

The more you can sincerely offer your child choices and stand aside as a neutral, loving guide, the more she will take responsibility for her own life. When kids really understand that their academic

> Grace: One of the best choices I ever made in planning my annual camp for homeschooled teenagers, Not Back to School Camp, was to make the first rule: "Attend camp only if you, personally, want to. Do not attend simply because your parents think you should." Any time a kid breaks another rule, which rarely happens (and again, we attribute that largely to our making sure that we don't have any unwilling participants), our approach to dealing with it flows out of this first rule. "Given that you choose to be part of our community here," we say, "we expect you to keep our agreements. Since you haven't, we need to find a way for you to make amends." No one has ever argued with us about that, and so we've had a pretty easy time handling discipline at camp.

 At the heart of Freedom is: CHOICE. Offer your child authentic choices in all possible areas. Invite children to make commitments, take on projects, and solve prob-lems. At the same time, expect children to keep their promises, and make the consequences of broken promises clear in advance.

learning is up to them, that their choices affect *them* more than they affect *you*, everything shifts. When they stop feeling that you are pushing on them, they will gradually relax their rebellious energy, decide what they want, and reach for it.

Freedom Strategies

- Give your children choices and explain the consequences. This is the freedom-loving alternative to giving orders and backing them up with threats. It creates more peaceful family relationships and, we believe, encourages more independence and responsibility in children. Here are examples of the choice/consequence approach:

  - Anna is ten years old and lives in a rural area, where she has been used to swimming in ponds and rivers with her friends. Although she is a good swimmer, her mother wants her to take swimming lessons this summer to improve her skills. Anna says she hates swimming lessons and refuses. Her mother says, "I am worried about your safety because as you get older, you will swim more and more without me or another adult being there. I am not willing to let you swim unsupervised unless you take swimming lessons. If you choose not to take swimming lessons, either you can swim only when an adult is present, or you can wear a life jacket when no adult is there."
  - Kayla is a senior in high school and has already been accepted to a selective state university. Senior slump seems to have hit her hard. Her father says, "Kayla, you are almost an adult, and letting your grades slide right now is up to you. However, I want you to know that it is possible you will lose your acceptance to college. It's happened to other kids. We can discuss what you will do if that happens, if you want. Let me know what you decide and how I can support you."
  - Eight-year-old Stephen wants to drop out of band because he is tired of practicing. His parents say, "You made a commitment to be in band and we rented you a violin. We would like

you to keep your promise. On the other hand, we do want this to remain your choice, and we can understand you are getting tired of practicing. From our experience, we think that if you decide to stick with it and give it your best shot, there's a very good chance you'll get a lot of enjoyment out of it and you'll be glad you did it, even though, as you're discovering, it's a lot of work. If you want to break your promise, you will need to tell your band director yourself, and then you will have to do extra chores to pay for the rest of the rental time. We are not willing to pay for an instrument that you aren't playing."

- Fourteen-year-old James wants to try homeschooling next year. His mother would like to support him in leaving school because he is bored, unchallenged, and tired of the social scene, which includes bullying and drugs. However, she works full time, and although she can do some of her work at home, she can't imagine how she'll find the time to work with James or supervise his studies. Together, she and James work out an agreement to try homeschooling for one semester, provided he comes up with an academic plan and a reading list on his own, works independently except when he needs specific help, and arranges to meet monthly with some of his former teachers so they can help monitor his progress. "I want to support you in working independently," his mother says, "but I won't push you. If you want to do this, you're going to have to be self-motivated." In addition, James will continue to participate in drama and soccer at school, an agreement he has worked out with the principal. Twice a week, he will spend a day in his mother's office, doing filing for a few hours in exchange for using one of the computers there for his studies the rest of the day. If James fails to keep his side of the deal, he goes back to school after Christmas.

In each of these examples, the child has an authentic, free choice to do what his parents prefer—or not. The parents openly state their preference, if they have one. In each case, if the child chooses not to do what his parents prefer, he will face consequences that are built in to the situation (called "natural consequences"—illustrated by Kayla's and James's situations) or that are understandably related to the situation (called "logical consequences"—as in Anna's and Stephen's stories). The parent here is acting as a "choice coach," in Thomas Armstrong's phrase, helping the child to anticipate and understand the consequences of possible choices.

- Where your superior wisdom and life experience must overrule the child's freedom, *then make it clear that the child does not have a choice.* Keep it simple. Don't pretend a choice exists where it doesn't! "I am unwilling to allow you to drive cross-country so soon after you getting your driver's license. We can discuss other possibilities for your trip." The fact of the matter is, you are the adult and are ultimately responsible for your child's well-being until you have completed the job of handing that responsibility over to the grown child. Plenty of autonomy and freedom—as we advocate—doesn't take away your responsibility or your right to pull rank when appropriate.

- Choose your battles carefully. That doesn't make children less compliant; in fact, it makes them more willing to accept your authority when exercised. Children get less compliant the *more* managed they are, not the other way around. If you give your eight-year-old a correction or order every five minutes, will she listen when you need to give her important instructions for being away from home? If you go to the mat over your teen's desire to dye his hair blue, will you have any influence left when he wants to smoke cigarettes? Many parents are afraid to give their children freedom on the unimportant issues, believing that they'll be more compliant when it comes to the important ones. We believe the reverse is true, and our experience supports this belief. The more aspects of a child's life you attempt to control, the more power struggles you'll have on your hands, and the less influence you'll have for the critical challenges. (You're the only judge of what's "important" or not. The only rule: *Everything* can't be important.)

- Set limits based on what *you* are and are not willing to permit, not based on an abstract theory about what's good for some hypothetical child. Children need limits. They don't really want to be more powerful than the adults around them—it's too scary. Just make your requirements simple, necessary, and *truthful.*

Believe it or not, you'll end up with a better relationship with your child if you say "I want you to go to bed by 9:30 P.M. because I need peace and quiet after that" than if you say, "You have to go to bed by 9:30 P.M. because it's good for you and that's what all eleven-year-olds do." Similarly: "You have to go to school because I can't think of anywhere else for you to go in the daytime and I'm afraid that if you don't, you won't learn academic subjects" is preferable to "Everybody has to go to school and you'll be a failure in life if you don't go." The problem with the second statement, which many adults assume is more compelling, is that (1) it's not true, and (2) most kids don't plan their lives quite that far in advance. (Neither do most adults!) Minimizing reasons and discussion around your decisions will help your child accept them. "I am responsible for your well-being, and I am unwilling to allow you to _____" is reason enough.

- Negotiate agreements. Keep your promises to your children, and they will accept that you expect them to keep theirs (both to you and to other people). "You made a promise, and I expect you to keep it" is more empowering than "Do it because I said so." If you break a promise to a child, apologize, repair any damage, and go on. If your child breaks a promise to you or someone else, instruct her to do the same. You don't have to be upset or disappointed; people do sometimes break their word. Treating your own and your children's promises with calm respect will teach them to take their own word seriously.
- Give plenty of downtime and autonomy where possible. Provide kids with "large doses of privacy and solitude," in John Taylor Gatto's words. Don't micromanage every aspect of your child's life. Trust. The more you do, the more evidence you will find that your child is trustworthy. The reverse is also true. Let children play. Play is the real work of childhood. Don't regiment their time too much, or fill it up with lessons and activities, or interrupt them continuously with instructions and requests.
- Be conscious of your own freedom. To really understand how to grant your children freedom, you have to start with yourself. Sometimes we see ourselves as victims rather than free agents. Most of us, overwhelmed by our obligations, often forget that we

made choices in the first place to live a certain way—to take on a challenging career, or get married or have kids, or even go on vacation. We too easily see ourselves as victims and focus more on the consequences of our choices than their benefits, losing sight of the fact that we face freedom each day: to choose new commitments or make changes in our lives. By becoming unconscious in this way about our own freedom, we make ourselves less helpful as freedom counselors to our children. But conversely, *the more self-aware we can become, the better guides we can be.*

Sometimes our difficulty in relating to our kids comes from our own self-doubt. We worry that they'll never get motivated to do anything beyond playing video games or eating potato chips—but truth is, we wouldn't worry about it so much if we weren't afraid, deep down, that we'd abuse any freedom we'd allow *ourselves*, that all *we* really want to do is vegetate. And sometimes that is all we—and our kids—want. So what? Is it any wonder that in these hectic times, we sometimes react by craving a serious break? Grace's busy professional singer friend, Carrie, took a long open-ended vacation recently and said, "All I want to do is sleep. And it doesn't let up. The more I relax, the more I realize how deeply tired I am." After a few months, she finally stopped feeling tired and went back to work recharged. But it didn't happen overnight—and in the end, she was glad she hadn't rushed herself.

The reality is: All of us have an inner slug and an inner dynamo.

Grace: I sometimes fantasize about taking six months to myself, living in a tiny, sterile apartment without a phone, without a job, doing nothing but reading magazines, ordering jewelry out of catalogs, and eating bacon and cherry pie and maple cream fudge. Is that really the life I choose for myself? No, far from it. But I've come to believe that the more I can be aware of how I feel conflicted, and accept my "lower" impulses, and even to some degree indulge them (every once in a while I spend a whole day reading magazines and catalogs in bed, every once in a while I have a junk-food binge), the more I can wholeheartedly choose to commit myself to "higher" goals.

Although we fantasize about doing nothing and may have binges of slothfulness, few of us would choose a whole life of that sort of inactivity for long. And, if we did, chances are it's because somewhere along the way, we felt really pressured to measure up to someone else's ideas of what we should be, and we've not yet made peace with that experience.

To get over your fear of slothfulness, we suggest that you make friends with it, with the creature inside who "abuses freedom." Indulge and work through your own desire to vegetate, and you'll be much more sane, humane, and effective in working with your kids. As most of us are now, our own inner guidance systems need recalibration. Exercise them, work them out, get the kinks out, dust them off . . . reclaim them as your own.

- *Relax.* Each thing we do—no matter how valuable—has an "opportunity cost": It costs us all of the things we are not doing or paying attention to while we are concentrating on this one thing. Does this mean we're doomed—that it costs too much to make choices—and that we should hang around in an eternal limbo? Of course not. But it does mean that we should all lighten up and stop buying our belief that there is a clear, hard dividing line between "good" choices and "bad" choices. Practice seeing the consequences of "good" choices as well as of "bad" ones. For instance, if you choose to excel at your work, the consequences may be that you don't have as much time for painting, playing

---

Michael Soguero: "The kids at my school who are viewed by the administration as 'committed to learning' have generally shut down on their natural curiosity. They are adept at school performance. Then I have other kids—one is building a boat at home and running competitively, the other reads science fiction nonstop and enjoys doing calculus in his head—these two are clearly following their passion and they're not doing well with the school demands. Most people on staff would not characterize them as committed to their learning. However, I think they enjoy a freedom to be themselves because their families support their uniqueness."

with your kids, talking to your parents on the phone, or pursuing a side career as a jazz singer or photographer. And similarly,
if your kids choose to focus on academic achievement, they
choose *not* to spend as much time reading library books on the
subjects that most interest them, or exploring caves, or talking
with friends or family, or gardening, or writing letters, or play-

---

Homeschooler Noam Sturmwind, seventeen, of British Columbia,
Canada, wrote us: "My parents have always given me plenty of solitude and freedom to pursue my interests and passions, while also
supporting me in other ways when I needed it. I believe this has
contributed a lot to my growth and love for learning and life in
general. I recall many examples over the years: playing outside for
hours on end, and learning about all the minute details in nature;
programming, experimenting, and playing around on the computer; reading just about anything I could get my hands on; and
experimenting with electronics, to name a few. I was never told that
I should be doing anything more educational or worthwhile. My
parents let me pursue whatever I was interested in at the time and
were genuinely interested when I wanted to show them something
I'd accomplished. This has continued through to today. Although
I have more obligations now, I still have a lot of freedom to follow
my interests. In the last few months I've been contracted to do
some computer programming—something that would not be possible if my parents hadn't given me the time and space I need for
that, including rearranging my around-the-house chores to give
me large blocks of uninterrupted time.

"One other time I was very glad to have a lot of space was a few
months ago, when I was going through a difficult period where I
had little motivation and was trying to figure out who I am and what
I want in life. After I explained to my parents that I needed to have
a lot of time to myself and why, they allowed me to have the space
to do 'nothing' all day— go for walks, read lots of fiction books, talk
with close friends about what was going on for me, and anything
else I felt up to doing, whether seemingly productive or not.

"I am very grateful to my parents for supporting me in this way,
and through them I've learned that it's okay to take the time to follow my own passions and interests in life."

ing the flute. Early readers may not learn to observe the natural world as directly or intimately as later readers do. Academic stars may not learn independence of mind.

- Let children commit themselves to their own goals. Then take their commitments seriously, and make it clear that you are available as much as your time and resources allow to provide the child with whatever support *he or she wants* (which is the subject of Chapter 8, "Support"). Many parents do the reverse: They try to make the child's choices for them, deciding what goals (including academic achievement) are worthy, spend their time and energy trying to manipulate the child into pursuing these goals, and neglect to provide support or show much interest in the child's *real* goals (which may be playing the guitar, raising snakes, surfing the Web, riding horses, meditating, doing karate, traveling . . .).

- Aspire to the self-discipline that grows naturally out of your desire to accomplish goals you set for yourself—and encourage that attitude in your children. "Discipline" can mean two things: order imposed on us by a more powerful authority, or order we choose for ourselves. Discipline is a good thing. (Lack of limits and guidance drives kids crazy.) However, too much imposed discipline can interfere with autonomy, cause emotional problems, and even interrupt the development of a child's sense of self. Guerrilla Learning parents seek to minimize the first kind of discipline while maximizing the second kind. The question is not *whether* to teach kids discipline but *how* to teach them discipline, and what costs attend different methods.

Susan Gushue: "One thing I love about D.C. Youth Orchestra is that the discipline is not imposed by some arbitrary authority. To learn the instrument you have to hold it a certain way, know how the measures work, etcetera. The kid understands that it's the thing that's imposing the order, not a person. When you have a master it's because there's something that you want, some thing of beauty that you aspire to. You've entrusted them to lead you where you want to be."

- Offer real choices whenever possible. Some parenting (and management) books advise that people should "feel" as if they have a choice. This is nonsense (if well intentioned). You can't fool a two-year-old more than once into "feeling" like she has a choice. A choice is real or not. Freedom is real or not. One thing human beings are brilliant at is knowing the difference between when they have freedom and when someone is trying to control them. (And any two-year-old will intuitively and automatically hone in on any pretense in an unauthentic "choice" by pushing you to your limit to see where you break.) Real choice means that your child might choose to do nothing—and that's because if people are free, they're free to make mistakes as well as to do noble things. Let your children confront the consequences of their choices. If a kid breaks a promise or disappoints a teacher or fails a course, the consequence will have more impact if unmediated by your preaching and moralizing. Children mostly just ignore and resist preaching and moralizing, just as you did when you were a kid. But they respect and wish to please adults who respect them.

- In each case, you have to ask yourself what you're really comfortable with or do what you have to do to *get* comfortable. But if you can willingly grant them, here are some possible choices your kids might benefit from. (Note: "Willingly grant" doesn't mean that you have to be 100 percent free and clear of conflict. It *does* mean that you're more than 50 percent in favor of trying such an experiment and that you're committed to sticking with your choice. It also may mean that you talk openly with your kids about your hesitation while affirming that you're interested in proceeding despite your concerns.) The examples that follow range from tiny to large, but they are listed in no particular order. What is "large" to us may be "tiny" to you. We hope they stimulate your imagination and help you think of more possibilities appropriate for your unique family.

  Aim for the top of class or just the middle.

  Choose what to excel at—and not necessarily have it be an academic subject.

Susan Gushue: "We offer our kids a 'mental health day' once every six weeks or so. The kids save up their mental health days for special activities. Sometimes they use them to get a chance to spend time alone with me or their dad. When Helen was eleven, she wanted to stay home one day when the twins were sick, just so she wouldn't be going to school alone. I encouraged her instead to think about what would be a really special use of her mental health day and to make her own choice. Helen finally decided to instead wait several weeks and stay home on a day she could go with us to the Goodwill Book Fair and buy used books.

Grace: Remember my story about learning ballet? When I was thirteen, and my mother noticed that I was stressed out, she asked whether I really wanted to be doing all that I was doing. In addition to attending school and church (neither of which was optional), did I also want to do gymnastics two to four times a week, go to ballet twice a week, and take weekly piano lessons? At that point, I made the choice to drop ballet. Just as starting, nine years earlier, had been my enthusiastic choice, stopping was also my clear—though reluctant—choice, and I felt well served by being allowed to think through my priorities and make the decision myself. The choice was mine and though I grieved, I never resented it.

Focus on the course of their choice and let others go.

Choose which electives to take.

Decide whether to focus on learning in or out of school. Or take it a step further: decide whether to attend school or homeschool.

Select what school to attend. For underchallenged teens, see if they'd like to take courses at a community college.

Flunk a class (or a grade) vs. pass it.

Decide whether to go on a family vacation, take music lessons, volunteer.

Choose whether to go to school on any particular day. Consider giving your kids a "well day" off from school once in a while, to pursue something they're really interested in. Ask them, though, to plan their "free days" well ahead of time, to make the most of them. They could go to a museum, spend the whole day reading, make a scrapbook, go on a long hike, or write. Or perhaps anxious, hurried, or overachieving children might choose to spend the day daydreaming, listening to music, or baking cookies. You will need to decide how you and your child want to handle this time off with the school. Amy prefers not to lie; when the school calls she says, "Carsie is staying home today." She doesn't offer an explanation. (But be aware: In most states school funding is tied to attendance, so when kids don't show up the school district loses money.)

Choose whether to study for a particular test.

Decide whether to do any particular homework assignment.

Think about whether to quit, or continue, something they're already doing.

- Then hold children accountable for the choices they've made—allow them to authentically confront the consequences, when possible. Often a gentle reminder that they have made a commitment is all that's required to help children work through

---

Randi Lewis: "I teach deaf kids, and one of the things I spend the most time teaching families is how to offer choices to their children, in the most basic way. I say to them, 'If you have five minutes to play with your child, ask your child to choose what to bring to you.' Some parents struggle with being able to offer even that most basic choice.

"Choice is very powerful. Ownership of anything is a way to accomplish something. When I go in with a new kid that I haven't tutored before, I let them know that it's their decision—if they don't choose to have me back, I won't be coming back. When I let them see that it's their decision—to choose to get help or continue to struggle—that's very powerful. The success level totally changes when kids have a choice."

Freedom Exercises

For you:

Think of something you've been struggling with in your life—trying to lose weight, or exercise, or start an exciting but scary project. See if you can give yourself some extra freedom in that area. Instead of just telling yourself you should do it, give yourself as much permission as you can muster not to do it. See how long you can keep it up, and notice what happens.

For your kids:

1. Is there something you've been in a power struggle with your child about? Start with something simple, like toothbrushing. Come up with a way to offer an authentic, even if simple, choice in the matter. For example: "Brandon, from now on, you can brush your teeth right after dinner if you want, which means you can't have a bedtime snack, but you'd get your brushing out of the way earlier. Or you can have a bedtime snack at 8:30 and then brush your teeth. You decide which one you want to do and let me know." See what happens. Treat it as an experiment—you're observing how your child's behavior changes when he's offered more freedom, not trying to win the power struggle.

2. Next, try offering a choice in a more important area. "I'd like to let you decide when to do your homework from now on. You can do it right after school, or after dinner, or get up early in the morning and do it. Which one do you think will work best for you?"

   Again, see what happens. The child may need to experiment with the results of different strategies, just as you are experimenting with the results of giving her more freedom. Often when the child makes a commitment, you will still need to be involved—but this time as a coach and support person, not as a boss.

temporary resistance. However, there's no sense in holding kids eternally captive to choices they've made in the distant (by their standards) past. As adults we sometimes change our minds—we get divorced, we drop our MBA program in favor of a counseling program, or we quit going to ballroom dance class because it's boring or we're too busy. While we do kids a service by holding them accountable to some degree to their choices, we do them a disservice by being completely rigid and inflexible—preventing them from, or punishing them for, quitting. Ultimately, quitting should be an acceptable option.

Resources

Holt, John. *Freedom and Beyond.* Portsmouth, NH: Heinemann, 1972, 1995.

Kvols, Kathryn. *Redirecting Children's Behavior.* Seatle, WA: Parenting Press, 1997.

Neill, A. S. *Summerhill,* revised ed. New York: St. Martin's Press, 1995.

See also our section on free schools in Appendix B.

8

Key #5

Support

I made my way back home through the darkening fields, to tell the family of my new discovery and of my meeting with Theodore. I hoped to see him again, for there were many things I wanted to ask him, but I felt it would be unlikely that he would have very much time to spare for me. I was mistaken, however, for two days later Leslie came back from an excursion into the town, and handed me a small parcel.

"Met that bearded johnny," he said laconically; "you know, that scientist bloke. Said this was for you."

Incredulously I stared at the parcel. Surely it couldn't be for me? There must be some mistake, for a great scientist would hardly bother to send me parcels. . . . I tore off the paper as quickly as I could. Inside was a small box and a letter.

My dear Gerry Durrell,

I wondered, after our conversation the other day, if it might not assist your investigations of the local natural history to have some form of magnifying instrument. I am therefore sending you this pocket microscope, in the hope that it will be of some use to you. . . .

With best wishes

Yours sincerely

Theo. Stephanides

P.S. If you have nothing better to do on Thursday, perhaps you would care to come to tea, and I could then show you some of my microscope slides.

—Zoologist Gerald Durrell, *My Family and Other Animals*

When you understand the power of offering your children authentic choices, you'll find that the energy you once spent on coercion must now be directed toward helping enthusiastic kids *achieve* their goals. Believe us—even if your child is inspired by something, it doesn't take any less effort! Children in passionate pursuit of a personal vision, whether it's winning the science fair, acing algebra, building a cage for a pet, getting into college, becoming a tap dancer or soccer player, or raising iguanas, usually need lots of adult support in the form of time, money, help, advice, chauffeuring, listening, hand-holding, and celebrating. But not to worry: Helping your child to create something will be satisfying and thrilling, in the end, for *both* of you. And we don't need to remind you of what you'll be missing: the frustration and disappointment that come with battling resistance.

There's no getting around it: It takes time and energy to really support your kids in their learning. Our approach—allowing kids as much freedom as possible to discover and pursue their own paths—doesn't mean you then abandon them to their own devices. Nor will you be able to get away with strategies like "quality time." Parents who take serious responsibility for their children's learning put in time, energy, and attention. And in most cases, as we've pointed out repeatedly, you don't have to speculate about what your kids might want and need—they will tell you.

Support is one major area in which Guerrilla Learning is different from "old-fashioned" (1960s-era) radical permissiveness. It's the critical element that prevents parents from, in the name of freedom, neglecting their kids. The experiments of many free schools and permissive families in the 1960s and 1970s revealed that unbridled leeway, in which parents were unwilling to set limits, drove kids bonkers. Like toddlers trying out their running skills by fleeing mom's arms yet still needing her when they fall, older kids need the security of wiser, more powerful, loving parents to set appropriate limits, pick them up when they fall, and—perhaps most important—*help them achieve their goals when they want and need help.* There is a critical distinction between attempting to force children to do something "for their own good," which is how many parents view their responsibility when it comes to education, and being lovingly available for help *when children request it.*

If the five keys are a theater production, support is the light crew, sound crew, makeup artist, costume designer, and stage crew—the invisible, behind-the-scenes structure that makes it possible for actors and singers to glisten in the colored lights. Sometimes (to extend the metaphor) support is the "audience" too. Although some kids do flourish on their own, and for a lot of kids it's better to make do with less nurturing attention if that means they win more precious autonomy in the bargain, the ideal situation *includes* loving, interested support. Most kids get either freedom or support, or neither—rarely a balanced and hefty portion of both.

THE FIVE PRINCIPLES OF SUPPORT

1. *Take care of yourself.*
2. *Make sure the goals are* theirs, *not yours.*
3. *Keep checking out how much support children need and want.*
4. *Help your kids identify their strengths and weaknesses.*
5. *Well-being comes first.*

Take Care of Yourself

Martyrdom is *not* support. Making conscious choices to allocate your precious time and energy to your children's projects is not the same as inappropriately sacrificing your needs for theirs. We are not advocating putting aside your own happiness or health or fulfillment for your children's. Yes, it's always a balancing act, as any parent knows. And yes, there are countless times when parents do, in fact, need to subordinate their own needs and desires to their children's. But in general, we recommend the goal of all family members' needs being met while they meet their obligations and pursue their interests. We've also found that when kids are wholeheartedly and generously supported in their projects and interests, they tend to be generous rather than competitive when it's *their* turn to support their parents.

It's important to acknowledge your limits. There may be some parents who live to do nothing but nurture their children, but we've never met them. Most of us can get excited about helping our kids for a certain amount of time, but at some point we want to stop. That point depends on a lot of things. In addition to our physical health and how busy our overall schedule is, it depends on how connected we feel to our kids, whether we are achieving our own goals, how grateful our kids are to us, how much we approve of their goals, how strong our relationships with other adults are, our financial situation, and other factors. We might indeed be better parents if we could just deal with these issues on our own, once and for all, and thus become more open to helping our kids. But in the meantime, while it's important to offer support to your kids, there's not some magical number of hours you must donate to their projects in order to ensure that they grow up to be joyful, lively creators.

Having become aware of your limits and having acknowledged them to yourself, *don't overdo it*. Don't overextend yourself. While you're gradually growing and becoming a more generous person, don't do any more than you're willing to do. Make only genuine offers. If all you can offer daily is a few minutes' worth of interest, encouragement, listening, and questioning, that's way better than making promises you can't keep or faking interest. And even a few minutes each day can be plenty—at least for some kids, some of the time.

In the parenting class Amy teaches, "Redirecting Children's Behavior," she uses the metaphor of airline safety to explain this principle to parents. Flight attendants explaining emergency procedures always instruct passengers traveling with small children that if the oxygen masks drop down, they should put their own mask on first, then help their children. Children need parents who are healthy and strong *first*. Then they can be helped and supported.

Make Sure the Goals Are *Theirs*, Not Yours

The simple, huge difference between support and pushing is who owns the goals. If you give your kids plenty of authentic freedom to make their own choices, you won't have to worry about whether or not you're pushing them, and they won't have to put a lot of energy into resisting, circumventing, or sabotaging your efforts to help. Nor will they later blame you for pressuring them into playing competitive sports, or forcing them to continue with piano, or pushing them to get into honors English. Give them real freedom to set their own goals and see what really inspires them. Contrary to some now-discredited reports, Tiger Woods' parents never pushed him to succeed in golf; in fact, his internal drive was so strong that his parents used it to coerce him into doing other things. (For example, his mother forbade him from hitting practice balls until he finished his homework—not an outstanding example of Guerrilla Learning, of course, but it illustrates our point.) Woods's parents made enormous sacrifices to help him achieve his goals but the goals were always his own.

Keep Checking Out How Much
Support Children Need and Want

Sometimes kids, especially teens, imply that they want you to give them a wide berth while secretly craving more attention. In reality, they probably crave *both* privacy *and* the assurance that you are seriously interested in them and what they're doing. Reach out to them. Ask how their projects are going, what they need, what they're up to in school and outside of it. Even when they rebuff you, don't presume that that means they never want your help. Seek the right balance here by making casual inquiries, honoring their wishes, and checking on them again tomorrow. Yesterday your fourteen-year-old daughter was brimming with self-confidence and cavalier about your offer to help with her clothing designs; today she's frustrated with the sewing machine, she ran out of lace trim, and she has nothing to wear to the concert tonight, but she's too proud to ask you for help. A casual repeat of yesterday's offer may be gratefully accepted today.

Amy and Grace both remember wishing as teens that someone would talk to them seriously about school—about what was confusing and what was exciting—but no one did. Neither one of them ever dreamed of asking; they were too busy trying to convince both themselves and their parents that they were grown-up and independent.

Grace: When I was about five, a question about parrots popped into my mind. I spoke the question aloud to my mother, who was stirring spices into a pot on the stove. I knew she was busy and when she answered, "I don't know, honey," I resigned myself to not finding out the answer to my question. A minute or so later, when she walked over to the bookshelf, it didn't occur to me that my question was still on her mind—truth is, even I wasn't thinking about it any more. But she pulled down the big *Birds of the World* book and said in a warm voice, "Let's see—parrots. . . ." That was a very bright moment for me, one in which I began to realize that my questions and my interests mattered to my parents, enough that my mom would actually set aside what she was doing in order to help me. That experience also helped me understand how much power I had in my family, and while I didn't feel any need to squelch my curiosity, I did begin to realize that I could do my parents a favor by being somewhat selective about what questions I asked aloud and making more efforts to find out the answers to my own questions, or at least think about them some before asking, or first consider whether they were important to me.

When you're truly feeling generous, you can do your kids a favor by letting them see that they rate high on your list of priorities. Obviously, helping your child is important simply because children need help with some things. But another invaluable aspect of support is the message it conveys to children that they and their interests are important.

Help Your Kids Identify Their Strengths and Weaknesses

One of the most exciting innovations to come out of education research in the last twenty years is Howard Gardner's multiple intelligences theory (referenced at the end of this chapter). Our culture once presumed that the smart folks were the ones good with words (reading, writing, debating, learning foreign languages) and logic (math, puzzles, computers, science). But Gardner's influential research has challenged that belief. Now, while most schools are still set up to emphasize and reward linguistic and logical thinking, we recognize other modes of intelligence, too, equally valid and useful: spatial, musical, body-kinesthetic, interpersonal, intrapersonal, and naturalist. The most user-friendly, enjoyable introduction to the multiple intelligences theory is Thomas Armstrong's 7 *Kinds of Smart.* (See "Support Resources.")

A related, somewhat simpler model of intelligence is the "learning styles" theory, which divides a person's learning style into three categories: auditory, visual, and kinesthetic. This theory proposes that people tend to learn using one—or sometimes two—dominant modes of absorbing and integrating information. Learning styles experts recommend that children be taught to learn "through" their dominant mode, thus building on strengths and achieving in school with less effort and heartache. Auditory learners do better when directions are given orally; visual learners can be encouraged to map out and illustrate their lessons; and kinesthetic learners, who often experience the most problems in school, learn best by doing—experimenting, demonstrating, and using three-dimensional materials.

By putting some time into studying and identifying your child's learning style, you can come up with strategies for working with nature instead of fighting it, while helping your child gradually to enhance his weaker modalities as well. For example, auditory learners learn to read best with phonics, visual children benefit from sight reading, and kinesthetic learners can be helped by tactile cues such as making letters out of clay or tracing them with the whole arm. (Armstrong suggests writing in the snow with colored water in a squeeze bottle for kinesthetic children!) Cheri Fuller's book, *Unlocking Your Child's Learning Potential,* is an excellent guide to learning styles (see "Support Resources") and includes a priceless chapter on "learning-different people who achieved," which illustrates dramatically how learning modalities that are considered weaknesses in school can be enormous strengths—and indicative of genius—in real life. Fuller's book is loaded with practical advice that can help you teach your kids to leverage their strengths to achieve in school while *managing* their weaknesses. The key is to find ways to change information into a form that they can easily grasp and remember.

Linda Silverman, Ph.D., who founded the Gifted Development Center in Denver(see "Support Resources" for information), has been exploring and documenting what she calls "Visual-Spatial Learners" for several decades. These can be children who "take the top off the IQ tests," according to Silverman, but can also be low-IQ scorers overall who are obviously bright and who far outperform other children on certain visual and spatial tasks. We believe Silverman's characterization of Visual-Spatial Learners—a group of kids who are extremely bright and yet often have the most trouble in school—will be useful to countless families:

> Visual-spatial learners are individuals who think in pictures rather than in words. They have a different brain organization than auditory-sequential learners. They learn better visually than auditorally. They learn all-at-once, and when the light bulb goes on, the learning is permanent. They do not learn from repetition and drill. They are whole-part learners who need to see the big picture first before they learn the details. They are nonsequential, which means that they do not learn in the step-by-step manner in which most teachers teach. They arrive at correct solutions without taking steps, so "show your work" may be impossible for them. They may have difficulty with the easy tasks, but show amazing ability with difficult, complex tasks. They are systems thinkers who can orchestrate large amounts of information from different domains, but they often miss the details. They tend to be organizationally impaired and unconscious about time. They are often gifted creatively, technologically, mathematically or emotionally. (See Support Resources for information on the Gifted Development Center.)

Observe which intelligences your child leans toward and which learning style she seems to favor. Make sure both that she has an opportunity to grow and shine in the areas of strength *and* that you offer nonthreatening support and encouragement to explore and grow in other realms. One way to address these issues is to seek out schools or classrooms that incorporate multiple intelligence or learning styles theory—or in which the teacher naturally emphasizes and rewards your child's intelligence and/or style.

But beyond the classroom, there's so much you can do. Provide plenty of challenge, recognition, and support for your child to build on strengths while including unpressured, incremental, welcoming "you-can-do-it" opportunities to master weaker areas as well. For instance: If your son is linguistically gifted and mathematically challenged, you might offer frequent trips to the library, a good bibliography describing great books, an introduction to a helpful librarian, a book or workshop for young people on how to get published, or trips to bookstores to hear authors speak or read. And at the same time, you might sit down and brainstorm with him, coming up with one or two simple ways to make math easier for him. Above all, let him know you're there for support. Specifically, you might suggest or offer a tutor, a good textbook designed to be used without a teacher's help, a study group, a computer tutorial, or your own help with homework. (And you'll also want to make it clear that you wouldn't just hire any tutor; you'd help him find one who made sense to him. You wouldn't just buy any book off the "math" shelf at the bookstore; you'd help him choose one that was clear to him.)

In other words, in relation to their strengths, you want to give your children the sense that the sky's the limit and that you'll help them reach their full potential—you won't let them run out of resources or mentors; you'll make sure that when they outgrow what they've got, you'll help them find more challenging and fulfilling opportunities. Furthermore, make sure your children have the opportunity to capitalize on their strengths. Especially with children who are gifted in nonlinguistic or analytic areas or are kinesthetic learners, beware of lecture-and-worksheet-centered classrooms, which reward linguistic and analytic intelligence while robbing kinesthetic learners of their self-confidence (and their educations). Fuller points out that most adults land in jobs that take advantage of their intelligences and learning styles—they don't force themselves into uncomfortable modes. Yet many children are forced into learning through their weakest modality for years on end.

We can all benefit from working on our weaknesses. Offer a welcoming, unpressured yet inspiring invitation: "Here is one simple step you can take, as soon as you are ready, that will help you begin to master valuable skills or information." But don't wait for kids to "fix" their weaknesses. They can learn, create, and be happily engaged in life and in learning *now*, especially if they are given room and encouragement to learn through their strongest modalities.

Pay attention to your own intelligences and learning styles as well. As with so many other parenting issues, trouble can be caused not so

much by each person's natural character but by a "bad match-up"—
a strongly auditory parent, for example, who can't understand why
her kinesthetic son won't listen to her verbal instructions for gathering the trash (she may learn to touch his arm when she speaks to him,
or perhaps act out her directions), or why her visual daughter ignores
her call while watching TV (she needs to get in front of the child and
wave!). As you become more aware of your own modality, you will

Amy: Carsie, like me, is a strongly auditory learner, although she has
enormous visual strengths as well (strengths I seem to lack—perhaps because I am legally blind without my glasses!). We're both
musicians, in fact; Carsie (unlike me) has perfect pitch. It was so
easy to teach her to read—we played spelling games in the car and
while working around the house, "reading" by stringing together
sounds: It was a totally auditory way to learn. When it was time to
link the sounds (auditory) to the letters (visual), everything just
clicked for her.

With Elijah, however, who is strongly kinesthetic and visual, it took
me a while to adapt my natural communication style. After working
with the alphabet for quite a while in school and at home, he still
didn't know the sounds of all the letters, and it bothered him. One
night Carsie (then fourteen) sat down with Elijah and together they
made a set of alphabet flash cards out of construction paper. Elijah
helped cut out each letter and paste it on a square of brightly colored paper. On the back of each letter, they pasted a picture of a *Star
Wars* character whose name began with that letter (Anakin, Boba
Fett, C3PO, Droid . . .), thus leveraging not only his learning style
but also his interests. The project of finding a character to match
each letter *alone* helped Elijah get the sounds down! The first game
we played was spelling very simple *Star Wars* character names, using
the letters ("HAN," "LUKE," "YODA . . . "). I noticed that Elijah
would sound out each letter, and say the word, but he still didn't
"feel" it—he didn't *know* he was reading, and I would see the frustration and helplessness arise in his face. I realized that it was his auditory weakness that was tripping him up, and I suggested he try to pay
attention to *his own voice.* "You're saying the word," I commented.
"You're just not listening to yourself!" That simple instruction made
a huge difference. As I became more and more conscious of Elijah's

kinesthetic orientation, I began to search for ways to make the experience even more tactile. One day, when his confidence in reading each name had grown and he had read a fairly long word, "SEBULBA" (the cheating pod racer from *Phantom Menace*), on an impulse I seized the seven letters, mixed them up, and handed them to Elijah. "Put them back in order—spell 'SEBULBA,'" I instructed. His eyes lit up as he approached the physical, spatial, touchy-feely task of arranging the bright, rough letters in order. I think he learned more "in his bones" about sequencing sounds from that exercise than from all the auditory directions I provided him in the past two years. His spatial and visual brilliance—the intelligence that allows him to follow diagrams for building complicated Lego structures that mystify me—kicked in and helped him read.

learn to adapt your communication style for each child. You also might pay attention to the style of your child's teacher and consider whether trouble is being caused by a bad match-up in the classroom. Most teaching in our schools is auditory and visual (although research indicates that *all* children benefit from a kinesthetic, or hands-on approach), and a strongly kinesthetic learner can benefit

Amy: When Brad and I separated, Carsie had just turned fourteen. Carsie and I had always been very close, and were used to talking things through. In addition, Carsie had a close, loving community of friends in whom she confided as well as a number of adults—family members and family friends—who were available for support. She wrote a story about her feelings about the separation, which was published in an education magazine, and I thought she was dealing well with her feelings. However, as the year after our separation wore on, Carsie became increasingly depressed, angry, and withdrawn, despite my attempts—and those of her father and other adults—to engage her in conversation. I finally asked if she would consider therapy, which she initially refused. Thankfully, several of her close friends also encouraged her to try therapy (and recommended a therapist they liked), and we found Carol, who saw us together and separately for six months. There were a number of hidden issues that Carol helped us to articulate, and the going was rough at times. I questioned myself as a parent; I agonized over my decision to end a twenty-two-year marriage; I experienced the pain of being unable to reach a child who had always trusted and relied on me before. In time, though, with Carol's help and with Carsie's courage and determination, our family has healed and stabilized, Carsie has begun to recover her self-confidence and develop her identity and authority as a young woman, and I, with much soul-searching, struggle, and prayer, have begun to find the path to self-forgiveness and the strength to build a new life for myself and my children.

enormously from simple changes in the classroom that allow her to move and touch and feel as she learns.

The larger advice we are getting at here is this: Get to know your kids well—not just "what they like" and what they know about themselves, but how they engage the world around them. Then offer situations, materials, and advice that support their particular natures. Multiple intelligences and learning styles are two of the most relevant frameworks for you to consider as a Guerrilla Learning parent. You also may want to think in terms of other paradigms—Ayurvedic types, Jungian types and archetypes, left/right brain theory, enneagrams, Meyers-Briggs types, and so on. See "Support Resources" for a list of books that offer various models of personality and intelligence.

Well-being Comes First

Few families sail through the vicissitudes of modern life without experiencing difficult periods during which social and emotional resources are strained to the point of breakdown. Whether the problem is one child hitting a temporary emotional bump in the developmental road or the entire family facing the heartbreak of a divorce, a death, or a financial crisis, all of us can be helped by a reminder that other healthy, loving families have troubles, too, and that outside help can be a blessing.

Sometimes there's no crisis or overt threat to a child's emotional well-being, yet parents long for help. What are effective ways to deal with the daily complexities of raising kids in a world vastly different from the one in which we grew up, without being overly rigid or overly permissive? Books that have helped us develop and hone our skills include *How to Talk So Kids Will Listen and Listen So Kids Will Talk* by Adele Faber and Elaine Mazlish. (See "Support Resources.") Faber and Mazlish's books give parents (and teachers) a powerful communication method that affirms children's feelings while eliciting their cooperation. Kathryn Kvols's *Redirecting Children's Behavior* (also in "Support Resources") provides strategies for affirming and encouraging the whole child, short-circuiting power struggles, and developing creative responses to demands for attention and helplessness. Another wonderful book is counselors Hugh and Gayle Prather's *Spiritual Parenting* (see "Support Resources"), which beautifully articulates an approach to parenting as a spiritual task (although you don't have to believe in God to read and enjoy it) that honors the deep, unique, divine nature of each child. All of these approaches provide ways to support children's emotional health and guide their behavior without harshness or excessive control.

 At the heart of Support is: RESOURCEFULNESS. Use your resources of time, money, expertise, experience, and loving attention to help your children achieve their goals. Guide them to other resources as needed. And take care of yourself—*you* are your children's most important resource!

SUPPORT STRATEGIES

Providing support takes a different form for a four-year-old and a twelve-year-old, differs even among two children of the same age, may even differ for the same child from month to month. Support requires something different depending on the interest: in swing dance vs. desire for school achievement vs. interest in horses. Yet regardless of the particular shape it takes, any really effective support grows out of a true desire to empower your kids. Here are some ways that desire might be expressed:

- Driving. If you already drive your kids around a lot, maybe you feel like it's a thankless task. Maybe it is. Maybe even you take yourself for granted. Nonetheless, it is a very real way to help your kids achieve their goals. If you're lucky, they'll grow up and have their own kids and finally appreciate you for all the driving you once did. Or maybe they'll clue in sooner. Grace remembers the little shock of awakening she had one day in high school when she and her friend Kris were waiting for Grace's mother to pick them up after gymnastics practice. Grace was annoyed that her mom was late; Kris, on the other hand, had a different perspective: "You're so lucky that your mom drives you to anything you want to get involved in. My parents don't do that." (P.S. Taking them to events they're interested in sometimes just means driving them, but other times you might choose to attend those events also.)

- Providing money for lessons, supplies, books, and the like when finances allow. Amy sometimes pays for her kids' interests and activities outright, and she sometimes provides "matching funds" —which requires the kids to demonstrate their commitment to the activity by sharing the expenses.
- Being a resource link—telling your kids about knowledgeable people, classes, events, books, and so on. When it's clear your child has a real interest in a subject, flip through your address book and see if you know anyone who's got expertise in that subject. Invite the friend over to dinner.
- Talking through your kids' plans and goals with them, being

---

Amy: Remember the mysterious shrimplike creatures mentioned earlier in our discussion on keeping a nature notebook? Carsie and some friends found them in a flooded backyard. The animals were about two inches long and totally transparent—you could see their guts working inside their bodies. They looked like colorless crayfish. No one around had ever seen them before. I knew a biologist at nearby Shenandoah National Park, so we called her. She couldn't identify the creatures, but she speculated that they were cavedwelling, since they were colorless, and perhaps had hatched from dry eggs and washed out from an underground cave when the yard flooded. Later we visited the National Zoo in Washington, and a very kind biologist named Chris there became fascinated with the creatures. He pored over resource books in his library until he figured it out. They turned out to be cave-dwelling freshwater relatives of brine shrimp—like the tiny creatures sold as sea monkeys in the back of comic books. (Later Carsie contacted Chris again—I helped her find the address—when some jellyfish she caught at the beach started glowing blue in their jars at night. "Yes, Carsie," Chris wrote back, "I looked it up: there is such as a thing as an electric comb jellyfish.") In each of these cases, Carsie might not have been able to find the people and resources she needed to help her research these creatures without my support. Yet I never "took the project over" from her; I just kept checking to see if she wanted more assistance.

their "choice coach," helping them to understand the potential consequences of their actions and choices.

- Being a "committed listener" for your kids. Often they just need a sounding board—someone to listen with full, loving, nonjudgmental attention. Practice listening without offering solutions.
- Getting "down and dirty" with them sometimes—donating elbow grease, companionship, plain old physical-realm help.
- Finding ways to build bridges between children and their dreams. If your small son says he wants to be a chef, help him

Randi Lewis: "My daughter is crazy and wild about reading. I have worked really hard in her school to get as many reading programs going as possible because that's her love. The school is using a very traditional curriculum—it's a lovely school and a very intellectual community with a lot of people who certainly respect education, but it's very traditional in its teaching methods. I did a lot of work in Sydney's class last year by starting a literacy circle. This year I started a 'Great Books' reading program and discussion group. We're really very excited about it. It's not for the so-called 'gifted' kids—I want it to be a heterogeneous grouping. One of the opportunities that kids have being in public school is the opportunity to be with kids who were raised differently and have different backgrounds."

make a special, beautiful cake or spend an hour together cutting vegetables into unique garnishes.

- Helping with stuff that you are much better equipped to do than they are, by virtue of your adult status and experience—for example, help them open a bank account for a business they want to start. Help them organize a study circle of people who share their interest in animal rights or computer programming. Use your skills on their behalf: fixing a bicycle, writing a brochure, sewing a costume. . . .
- Teaching them skills you know.

Omar Collins: "When our son Hanif was in fifth grade in public school, the class was studying the Constitution. His teacher made the comment that kids did not have rights. My son took exception to this, and was shot down—basically, she told him to be quiet. Hanif, who has a strong sense of justice, came home that day with a group of kids who started researching the question. They went to the library, they read the Constitution, they put together a report. Personally, I thought the teacher was just baiting them by refusing to discuss the issue—trying to 'hook' them so they would get engaged. But she wasn't; she was dead serious. The next day at school, Hanif tried to present their position to her, and she told them to be quiet, that they had to finish the unit on the Constitution. When she finally let him speak, he argued that the Constitution doesn't say anything about ages, it says if you're born a citizen you have certain inalienable rights. She said no, you're wrong. She was angry and (I believe) felt her authority was threatened. Hanif was very upset, and I spoke to the teacher about it. Eventually the principal found out about the incident. After hearing all sides, he requested that the teacher apologize to the class for refusing to take their project seriously. He commented to her, 'You have lost your class.'

"The teacher still resented Hanif, though, and we ended up requesting that he be transferred into another class, which he was. That teacher loved his enthusiasm and curiosity, and he had a great year."

> **Lisa Dunn:** "My son, Jack, was coming home from school this year [second grade] upset because he felt his teacher was insulting his work. I originally tried to empower him so that he could tell her how he felt. As time went on, he couldn't talk to her candidly, so I did the talking for him and spoke to her. His teacher was very receptive and opened the discussion up with Jack. Their relationship has improved. I just hope if something arises for Jack in the future he will know he is allowed to respectfully tell an adult he doesn't like how he is being treated."

- Not being too busy for them. Sometimes *don't* say "Just a minute, honey"; set aside what you're doing *right now.*
- Encouraging them to think about, and ask for, what they want.
- Asking other people for things on their behalf.
- Asking questions—take an active, loving interest in them. Read drafts of their short stories, ask if you can see how their fort is coming along, request a sneak preview of the Web site they're working on.
- Exploring your kids' and your own intelligences and learning styles. Teach them to transform information into their favorite form—auditory learners can tape lessons and listen to them; visual learners can make charts and "mind maps"; kinesthetic learners can make models of information.
- Participating in their classrooms. Today's teachers are under pressure from many different directions. Strengthening your relationship with their teachers benefits kids, teachers, and you. In addition, working to bring outside resources and creativity to classrooms is one way you can share your Guerrilla Learning passions with other children and the whole community.
- Advocating for them at school. Of course, no parent wants to be guilty of fighting a fight on behalf of a child who is clearly in the wrong or making things harder on teachers. Any dispute with teachers or administration must be carefully talked out to tease out the real issues. Adele Faber and Elaine Mazlish's *How to Talk So Kids Can Learn* (see "Support Resources") contains a very useful chapter on how to communicate with teachers in a positive way that doesn't offend or provoke defensiveness. Just be sure

that when your intuition tells you that a child needs your faith and support—even if you're risking making the wrong decision—you support your child, acknowledge her feelings, and help her find a way to solve the problem.

- In supporting your child's interests, don't limit yourself to academics or interests that coincide with your own. If your son is interested in both geometry and hair cutting, and you happen to think that hair cutting is a shallow or worthless pursuit, see if you can find it in your heart to invite both your own hairstylist and your math professor friend to dinner (on the same or different nights—your call!). Let your kids know that you support

---

Support Exercises

For you:

1. In a journal or just in your own mind, reflect on how you were supported in your interests as a child. How did your parents, teachers, siblings, or others help and empower you to achieve your goals? And how did they get in your way or fail to support you? How do you feel about all of that now? Bitter? Grateful? Sad? Angry? Full and happy? A mixture of conflicting emotions? Recall a time in your life when you had passionate dreams or goals. What do you wish your parents or other adults had done, or given, to support your dreams? Is it too late? Can you give yourself these things now or ask someone else to give them to you? Are you moved to thank a parent or other adult now?

2. Choose an interest you'd like to pursue—maybe one of the interests you've worked with in a previous chapter. Think of a way you'd like help from someone you know—spouse, friend, kid, relative, neighbor. For instance, you might want them to:

- Let you pick their brain
- Check in with you frequently to see if you're meeting your own goals

- Listen to you talk about what you're doing, and make appropriately impressed noises and comments
- Lend you stuff
- Lend or give you money
- Teach you something

Now ask for what you want. If they say no, ask someone else, or revise your request and ask the same person again. Practice asking until you get to "yes." Notice your own feelings about asking for and about accepting help.

For your kids:

1. Choose one of your kid's biggest interests. Generate a list of ways you could offer support. Tell your children to pick one or two things from your list to start, and that you want them to ask for your help. The point here is not only to give your kids these particular kinds of assistance but also to help them develop their ability to notice what they want and ask for it.

2. Choose another of your kid's interests—something you have a hard time accepting. Grace once read a religious advice column that boiled down to something like this—*Q*: "What if I don't love my husband anymore?" *A*: "Make him his favorite breakfast every morning. Smile and kiss him more than ever. Say to yourself, 'How would I treat him if I did love him?' and then do those things. Basically, *act* as if you love him, and soon you'll find that you really *do*." Now, we're not sure that's always good advice for an ailing marriage. But we do think it's worth experimenting with in a lot of different contexts and certainly worth translating into the "what to do when you don't approve of your kids' interests" realm. Ask yourself: What would you do if you thought it was completely awesome that your daughter's favorite pastime was reading *Sweet Valley High* books? Maybe you'd buy her the next one that came out, or ask her to read her favorite out loud to you, or try to get an autographed copy for her, or perhaps just ask her what she liked about them.

their learning and interests because you love them, not because you want to control them.

- Keep your eye out for events, newspaper clippings, museum exhibits, and the like related to your child's interests. Present these in the spirit of "just passing along useful information," not with the agenda that she necessarily follow up on any of it. If you can't honestly offer it in that spirit, don't do it. Or give your child a gift certificate to a store or catalog that sells products related to his interest.

- Plan a family weekend or a vacation/trip around one of your child's interests. Involve him in the planning—don't make him feel that you're taking over his territory. You may be surprised at how receptive museum staff can be to an enthusiastic child. Amy's family has taken trips focused on marine biology, Civil War battle reenactments, and horse shows. Carsie has been invited "backstage" to witness the behind-the-scenes activity at the National Aquarium in Baltimore, the Invertebrate Laboratory of the National Zoo, and the Marine Museum in Solomons Island, Maryland. Moved by her enthusiasm about marine animals (which occupied her from the age of seven to around eleven), staff people have let her participate in feeding animals, showed her around, and discussed her projects with her. When they were eleven, Carsie and her friend Charles found an inexpensive, conservation-related weeklong summer day camp run by the Nature Conservancy in Nags Head, North Carolina, and both their families made a vacation of it by driving down for the week and renting a house nearby.

- Help your kids go to a good, large library and check out recent books on a subject they're interested in. Libraries also have specialized magazines on lots of different subjects, CDs, books on tape, videos, computers with Web access, printers, and copiers. And help your kids use the Internet to connect with people all over the world who are passionate and experienced in the fields they want to research. Newsgroups or bulletin boards actually can be better for this than the Web. You and your kids may find that the information available in the real world is very different from how the subject is presented in school materials. School textbooks are often out of date, plus they have to be approved by committees and acceptable to a diverse constituency with conflicting interests in different states. The result is blandness. Often you won't find controversial or even cutting-edge information in them.

Resources

Armstrong, Thomas. 7 *Kinds of Smart: Identifying and Developing Your Many Intelligences.* New York: Plume, 1993.

———. *The Myth of the ADD Child: 50 Ways to Improve Your Child's Behavior and Attention Span without Drugs, Labels, or Coercion.* New York: Plume, 1997.

Faber, Adele, and Elaine Mazlish. *How to Talk So Kids Can Learn.* New York: Rawson Associates/Scribner, 1995.

———. *How to Talk So Kids Will Listen and Listen So Kids Will Talk.* New York: Rawson, Wade Publishers, 1980.

Frager, Robert, ed. *Who Am I? Personality Types for Self-Discovery.* New York: Putnam, 1994.

Fuller, Cheri. *Unlocking Your Child's Learning Potential.* Colorado Springs, CO: Piñon Press, 1994.

Gardner, Howard. *Frames of Mind: The Theory of Multiple Intelligences,* Tenth Anniversary ed. New York: Basic Books, 1983.

Godwin, Malcolm. *Who Are You? 101 Ways of Seeing Yourself.* New York: Penguin, 2000.

Kvols, Kathryn. *Redirecting Children's Behavior.* Seattle, WA: Parenting Press, 1997.

Prather, Hugh and Gayle. *Spiritual Parenting: A Guide to Understanding and Nurturing the Heart of Your Child.* New York: Random House, 1996.

Silverman, L. K. "Upside-Down Brilliance: The Visual-Spatial Learner," (publication pending), copyright © 2001 by L. K. Silverman.

Tieger, Paul D., and Barbara Barron-Tieger. *Nurture by Nature: Understand Your Child's Personality Type—And Become a Better Parent.* Boston: Little, Brown, 1997.

For more information about Visual-Spatial learners, contact:
The Gifted Development Center
1452 Marion Street
Denver, Colorado 80218
303-837-8378
www.gifteddevelopment.com

Afterword
A More Beautiful Question

The creative is found in anyone who is prepared for surprise.
—James P. Carse, *Finite and Infinite Games*

Education is not a race, with winners and losers. It's not a commodity to be bought and sold. It can't be measured, not in test scores or in degrees. Although it has many uses, it has no real purpose beyond the joy it produces. It doesn't belong to anyone. It's never over. If education is a game, it's a game that anyone can play, that doesn't end, and that gets better each time a new player joins. It's an "infinite game," to use a phrase by James Carse—a game the purpose of which is to keep playing.

School achievement is *not* education. Obedience is *not* education. Scoring high on a test is *not* education. There's nothing wrong with school achievement, obedience, or high test scores, except when they get in the way of real learning.

True education occurs whenever a free human being responds to the magnificent world with wonder, with fascination, and with the full and mysterious power of the human heart and mind to understand. This can happen in solitude or in company. It can last for a minute or for a lifetime. It can be spontaneous or inspired, but it can never be coerced. It is every child's right.

We close with a few lines from the poet e.e. cummings:

. . . never to rest and never to have: only to grow.
Always the beautiful answer who asks a more beautiful question

Appendix A

Testing Our Patience

Standardized Testing in the School System

Insanity is doing the same thing over and over
again expecting a different result.
—Author Rita Mae Brown, *Rubyfruit Jungle*

Big bureaucracies, such as state and national education authorities, have a management problem. They want to know whether the money they are spending on schools is being well spent. Are children learning what they're supposed to learn? Are things getting better or worse? How do schools in different areas, with different amounts of funding, compare to one another?

In order to answer those questions—how *are* the schools doing?—bureaucrats turn to testing experts, who devise tests for kids to take. One ubiquitous test is the *standardized test,* in which a group of children is tested and their scores are considered to be "normal," or the "standard," for purposes of comparison. Future groups of test takers are compared to the original group. That way bureaucrats can figure out whether kids are doing better or worse compared to the original group.

Standardized tests are *not* designed to evaluate the educational achievements of one individual child. That's why you don't get the "wrong answers" back on the Iowa Basic Skills Test so you can help straighten out your child's mistakes. Standardized tests really evaluate the school, or a group of schools.

Many teachers don't know that. Many parents don't know that. Of course, hardly any children know that the test they're sweating over is supposed to be assessing their school, not them.

Another kind of test is the "minimum competency test," which *is* designed to evaluate the progress of individual children. In response to a national concern with supposed low educational achievement in this country, more and more states have implemented minimum competency tests at various grade levels to make sure children have learned what they are supposed to learn before progressing to the next grade or level. In many states children can no longer graduate from high school without passing a competency test. Because of the high risk associated with taking these tests—the risk of being held back, not graduating, or being required to take extra coursework—this recent practice of linking school progression with a single test is sometimes referred to as high-stakes testing. Proponents of these tests claim that they will encourage high academic *standards*, and recently there has been much political dialogue about standards. However, parents should be aware that *standardized testing* and *standards* are two different things.

The high-stakes-testing, back-to-basics, pro-standards atmosphere in today's classrooms is not a result of the bureaucratic attempt to track schools' progress over time and distance to which standardized testing has been a solution. Today's atmosphere is the result of high-profile government reports, beginning with "A Nation at Risk,"[1] which claimed American kids' test scores were declining, our schools were getting worse, our kids were not keeping up with kids in other countries, and our economy (at the time of the report) was in trouble as a result. Many critics have since questioned the methods and conclusions of "A Nation at Risk" and other high-publicity efforts to encourage crisis rhetoric.

Among other real difficulties in drawing broad conclusions about American student achievement are: the numbers and backgrounds of the kids taking the tests (as with the SATs) have changed dramati-

---

[1] National Commission on Excellence in Education, *A Nation At Risk: The Imperative for Education Reform*, April 1983.

cally over the last fifty years, making it impossible to compare scores meaningfully; standardized tests are renormed periodically, making broad comparisons over many years difficult; and the American student population is exceedingly diverse compared to the populations of other countries, where, for example, teachers don't have to worry about students who speak dozens of other languages besides that spoken in the classroom. For a thorough, objective analysis of what the actual statistical evidence says and does not say about American school performance, see *The Way We Were?: The Myths and Realities of America's Student Achievement* by Richard Rothstein (in "Testing Resources").

(Note: Both standardized and minimum-competency tests are different from everyday classroom quizzes, which are intended to assess a student's grasp of covered material for the purpose of review and midcourse corrections, or from exams, which measure how well the student absorbed the course material over various blocks of time.)

Here is one weakness of both of these kinds of testing: *Research has demonstrated repeatedly that correct answers on a test do not necessarily represent real learning. Nor do they predict either academic achievement or real-life achievement.* As discussed in Chapter 1, testing tends to measure "decontextualized" information, or data with no context, no understanding of how the facts relate to each other or to the larger subject. Measures of deeper knowledge—the kind that outlasts the test—are harder to come up with.

A second problem is that, under predictable pressure to provide evidence of achievement, schools tend to swap the means with the ends. As high-stakes testing opponent (and authentic education proponent) Alfie Kohn has pointed out, teach-to-the-test activities routinely displace higher-level learning opportunities. Instead of working harder and harder to offer deep knowledge, schools, being systems, tend to work harder and harder to improve the *appearance* of knowledge: to raise test scores. Pressure builds to teach to the test, favoring rote memorization and superficial thinking. The symptom—low test scores—is treated as if it were the disease—poor education—and all efforts are concentrated on resolving the symptom. When test scores inevitably rise as a result of all this test-coaching, guess what testing proponents conclude: that rising test scores prove their programs work!

U.S. Senator Paul D. Wellstone, a former college professor, in a speech to Columbia University's Teachers College in March of 2000, characterized high-stakes testing as stressful, unfair, and "a failure of moral imagination" on the part of policymakers. "It is as though people are saying, 'If we test them, they will perform,'" said Wellstone. "In too many places, testing . . . has ceased its purpose of measuring educational and school improvement and has become synonymous with it." Wellstone pointed out that even the test publishers themselves consistently warn against the practice of making important decisions based on children's scores on a single test.[2]

Ironically, teachers and principals in high-stakes-testing states are increasingly being punished for cheating (by giving away test questions)[3] when, in a way, spending the whole year preparing kids to take a test that's supposed to measure what they learned *is* a kind of cheating. The ones who get fired are just cheating in a less acceptable way!

Critics of high-stakes testing also condemn the idea that a single written test can effectively measure a student's progress over a year, or—as in Virginia's Standards of Learning test, one of the nation's strictest—two or three years. Good test takers are rewarded; teaching to the test is rewarded; kids with learning styles that tend to match the kinds of knowledge that can be measured by multiple-choice testing are rewarded. Many kids (and teachers)—those who succeed as well as those who fail—are stressed out, demoralized, turned off, and uninspired as a result.

Others contest the very idea of a centralized authority that dictates how and what teachers teach.[4] Such a centralized authority sets up a bad model for students because it doesn't allow teachers to emerge as thoughtful, accountable adults, seriously engaged with the dynamics of their own schools, classrooms, and communities.

"As it stands today," writes Leon Botstein, president of Bard

---

[2] U.S. Senator Paul D. Wellstone, : "High Stakes Tests: A Harsh Agenda for America's Children," Teachers College, Columbia University, March 31, 2000.

[3] See, for example, "School Allegedly Cheated on Tests—Principal in Potomac Resigns over Md. Achievement Exams," *Washington Post,* June 1, 2000.

[4] Deborah Meier makes this case in *Will Standards Save Public Education?* (Boston: Beacon Press, 2000).

College in New York, "testing is little more than an adult political obsession that just results in more tests and profits for test makers . . . The most egregious aspect of our mania for testing is that pupils never find out what they got wrong and why they got it wrong. . . . Even the teachers don't get the results back in time to help them in their classrooms."[5]

Further, the tests, and much of the kind of get-tough-on-education thinking that produces them, often disregard basic realities about how kids grow and learn. Fourth-grade teacher John Palm writes:

> The Washington Assessment of Student Learning (WASL) has, in its three-year life, shown itself to be not only a colossal waste of money, time and effort. . . . As a fourth-grade teacher, I have learned that the WASL is poorly-designed and the level of difficulty is absurdly high. Fourth-graders are asked to perform reasoning tasks that are too advanced for 10-year-olds, making the WASL developmentally inappropriate. Its supporters applaud 'setting the bar high.' How silly! Have the track coaches taken control of our schools?"[6]

One of the most serious threats of high-stakes testing is its toll on the emotional lives of its "victims." While adults argue about the meaning of various forms of statistical measurement and the relationship between what happens in public elementary schools and the health of the economy, the question for children is not theoretical, but real and pressing. Leonard Turton, a sixth-grade teacher who asked us not to mention his city and school, posted this e-mail on an Internet list for educators:

> I have to put my grade 6's through "the test" . . . I keep it low-key and do whatever I can to downplay it. Today we did a bit of practice, slowly, together, using an old test, in as nonthreatening a way as I could possibly offer. The context of the questions, the language, the set-up is so foreign to what is in their textbooks or to how an 11-year-old thinks

[5] Leon Botstein, "A Tyranny of Standardized Tests" (editorial), *New York Times*, May 28, 2000.

[6] John Palm, "WASL is Trojan Horse for School Control" (editorial), *Seattle Times*, May 11, 2000.

and learns that by the end of this "tame," light session, three kids had resorted to staring into space and scribbling back and forth on their papers and another one collapsed into tears . . . ten more were in shock. Our tests go on for two and a half hours a day for five days.

The math covers the whole year, with no benefit of review (we aren't trusted to have the test for any meaningful time before we administer it), so if you have great long-term memory you have a chance. It's all language driven, so the "hands-on" kids are immediate failures.

The main thing you see is self-esteem being kicked in the gut. It's a horrible experience for a teacher. These are inner city kids with poor and fragile egos with lots of life failures. . . . I feel like a gestapo agent.

Pretend you are in university . . . suddenly, in the math course, you have a six-hour exam on the whole year's work with no chance to review . . . and they are doing this to eleven-year-olds. Younger kids have been known to stab their desks and tests repeatedly with a pencil or go into a depressed slump, or cry during the tests and at home, or rip their papers up, or simply refuse to do them.

So who started this? Who are these people who know nothing about children, children's learning, about people management or motivation skills?

You or I would never do such things to our own children, but we are allowing it to be done to them by others. Let's cut to the chase: this is not just a policy disagreement. This isn't about making sure schools are working. Something is very evil here, almost revengeful. . . .

Jennifer Oman, a first-grade teacher on a Hopi Indian Reservation, responded:

I had to cry after reading [Leonard Turton's letter], because I have just lived through the horror of administering the [California] Stan 9 test to my students. We were forced to give the entire test in three days, testing up until 2:00 P.M.. My students were so depressed and demoralized. We have worked so hard all year, and to be judged by this unfair, inhumane and culturally biased test was quite depressing. I feel that there is madness in public education. . . .

The high-stakes testing political drama is propelled by the rhetoric of people who believe that schools should be accountable for their results the way big businesses are accountable to stockholders for their profits. "Let's just figure out what kids are supposed to learn, measure it at the end, and punish those schools who aren't successfully imparting it! How hard could that be?" is the general idea. It's the free-market, bottom-line, hard-nosed idealism that pervaded public discussion in the "neo-conservative" 1980s and 1990s, applied to education.

But kids aren't products, schools aren't businesses, and human beings are notoriously harder to manage, quantify, and measure than nonhuman entities. Education happens in the *unmeasurable* connection between a child and a teacher, a child and a parent, a child and a book, a child and the wondrous, complex, astonishing, mysterious world. If teachers are not able to fine-tune for each child, each class, each school, in different months, seasons, and years, they are not teaching but programming—*training* kids to choose the right answer. If children have no freedom to interact with the world of knowledge according to their particular rhythms, their interests, their family's background, and the subculture in which they live, too often their love of learning and their ability to be creative, thoughtful, joyful citizens of a free society will be inhibited.

Despite reports to the contrary, it is downright impossible to assess human beings scientifically. Human beings are not like the rest of the material world or like other animals whose behavior can be objectively quantified and predicted. Human beings are free, which means that, to one extent or another, their behavior is not contingent on circumstance. They are always able to surprise both you *and* themselves.

The opinions of twenty experts about how your child is doing are not necessarily worth as much as *your* subjective intuition, based on your sensitivity, your vast experience of your child, and love. That's not to say you shouldn't consult experts if you are at a loss—just that you should take their opinions, based on made-up if useful models of human behavior, with many grains of salt.

In the past twenty years a number of alternative models of assessment have evolved and been invented—ways that parents and teachers can get useful information on children's schoolwork: what they've learned, what they've created, and what they need to do next. Many people are working to get those alternative assessment methods put into practice in classrooms instead of tests and grades. In the meantime, though, here's what you can do.

Testing Strategies

- Familiarize yourself with the various tests—standardized and high-stakes—that are being given in your state and locality. Look into the kinds of learning being measured, the amount of preparation that teachers are investing, and the consequences of various results for your child, teachers, and schools. Many parents focus by default on the scores and experiences of their individual child rather than looking at the bigger picture in which many children are not being served.
- If your child doesn't test well, has a great deal of anxiety, seems overly stressed, or just objects to the boring, decontextualized, drill-and-kill hours spent preparing for the tests, address the problem creatively. In some states you can file a waiver that excuses your child from testing. In addition, parents, students, and teachers in many states are organizing to resist high-stakes testing. (There are also well-organized groups of parents in favor of the standards movement and high-stakes testing.) Students have staged walkouts in some areas. Teachers are quitting in protest. Many teachers take the attitude "This too shall pass" yet are concerned about the effects on today's children whose school hours must be diverted to test preparation and test-taking. See "Testing Resources" for organizations that can help you resist testing or join the antitesting movement.
- If you are so inclined, educate yourself about alternative forms of assessment and advocate for them at your school. Alternative assessment—portfolios, teacher observations, projects, and so on—provides far richer, more useful, and some say fairer information than test scores. FairTest (listed in "Testing Resources") is an organization that promotes alternative assessment.

- Help your children deal with the stress of testing. Encourage them to get exercise and get outdoors, eat well, and get plenty of sleep. Meditation can help.
- Offer to help your children learn simple study techniques that can make them better test takers. Here is one potential attitude that can help: "This test is a game. Let's try to win. However, let's remember that it's only a game, it doesn't really matter, and it certainly doesn't tell us anything really meaningful about who you are or what you know."
- Don't let panic about academic achievement ruin your child's life, spoil your family life, or get in the way of real learning.
- Don't "buy in" to the national panic about standards, achievement, or competition. In one of those common, mystifying ironies of political life, people who are *actually* well educated question the methods and conclusions of the "education crisis" rhetoric, which is mostly propaganda masquerading as science.

Testing Resources

Kohn, Alfie. *The Case Against Standardized Testing: Raising the Scores, Ruining the Schools.* Portsmouth, NH: Heinemann, 2000.

———. *The Schools Our Children Deserve: Moving Beyond Traditional Classrooms and Tougher Standards.* New York: Houghton Mifflin, 1999.

Alfie Kohn is keeping track of parents and teachers organizing to oppose high-stakes testing. Go to www.alfiekohn.org for a contact number in your state.

McNeil, Linda. *Contradictions of School Reform: Educational Costs of Standardized Testing.* New York: Routledge, 2000.

Ohanian, Susan. *One Size Fits Few: The Folly of Educational Standards.* Portsmouth, NH: Heinemann, 1999.

Rothstein, Richard. *The Way We Were?: The Myths and Realities of America's Student Achievement.* Washington, DC: The Twentieth Century Fund Press, 1998.

Sacks, Peter. *Standardized Minds: The High Price of America's Testing Culture and What We Can Do to Change It.* Reading, MA: Perseus Press, 2000.

The National Center for Fair & Open Testing (FairTest) is an advocacy organization working to end the abuses, misuses, and flaws of standardized testing and to ensure that evaluation of students and workers is fair, open, and educationally sound.

FairTest
342 Broadway
Cambridge, MA 02139
617-864-4810
www.fairtest.org

Appendix B
Alternatives to Traditional Schooling

The future of Summerhill itself may be of little import. But the future of
the Summerhill idea is of the greatest importance to humanity. New
generations must be given the chance to grow in freedom. The bestowal
of freedom is the bestowal of love. And only love can save the world.
—A. S. Neill, *Summerhill: A Radical Approach to Education*

UNDERCHALLENGED IN HIGH SCHOOL

If your kids are bored or unchallenged in high school, they might
take all or part of their course load at a community college. Many
states permit high school students to attend community college part
time, while taking some high school courses at the high school or at
the college. At the end of their senior year, they're given a diploma
and have accumulated some college credit as well. Many teens find
that these college courses are more fun, interesting, and challenging
than those in high school. Don't assume that their grades are too bad
or that they're not the "type" who participates in this kind of program. Also, don't assume that community college courses aren't as
good as those at universities. Many community college teachers teach
because they love their subject and love to teach, unlike university

professors, who sometimes view teaching undergraduates as an unfortunate requirement of their real job, which is writing and doing research.

If your high school principal refuses to agree or if your state law prevents children from receiving high school diplomas under these circumstances, don't give up. The best-kept schooling secret of all is this: *You don't necessarily need a high school diploma to get into a four-year university.* Talk to the admissions officer at the colleges your child is interested in attending. Depending on the school, your child may be admitted without a diploma, based on existing high school credit, community college attendance, outside activities such as volunteering and sports, and SAT scores. Colleges that recruit homeschoolers or alternative school graduates are good candidates.

Also, some states have vocational ed programs that allow you to work at a kind of internship in your field while taking classes over the Web.

GUERRILLA LEARNING SCHOOLS

Some schools that are compatible with Guerrilla Learning principles, and in which you can expect to find consistent kindness toward children, respect for developmental realities, a natural incorporation of different styles and modes of learning, and a reverence for deep knowledge, are the following:

Waldorf Education

Waldorf schools were designed by Austrian philosopher Rudolf Steiner (1861–1925) to educate children consistent with what he viewed as spiritual reality and the ideal development of children's physical, emotional, and intellectual lives. Waldorf schools emphasize movement, the arts, crafts, and music as well as the gradual, developmentally appropriate introduction of intellectual material. A strong teacher/child bond is fostered and respected, teachers are given a great deal of independence, and one teacher usually stays with one class until high school. Arts and practical skills are viewed not as luxuries but as fundamental to learning and development. An atmosphere of deep respect for the child and for the beauty of culture and nature pervades the classroom. Discipline is handled between the teacher, the child, and the parent rather than delegated to administrative authorities.

For more information on Waldorf schools, check out www.waldorf world.org or www.aswna.org or contact:

Association of Waldorf Schools of North America (ASWNA)
3911 Bannister Road
Fair Oaks, CA 95628
916-961-0927

Montessori

Developed by Maria Montessori (1870–1952), Italy's first female physician, Montessori schools provide a structured setting that encourages children to learn through direct, interest-initiated interaction with the special materials and the environment rather than through texts or verbal instruction. Montessori schools in this country have predominantly been preschools, but more and more elementary-school and even middle school Montessori programs are emerging. Children in these schools are viewed as being eager and willing to learn, provided the right materials are offered and adults mostly stay out of the way. Montessori offers a certain amount of freedom, albeit within limits. Children are placed in multiage groups and are relatively free to pursue tasks of their own choosing during the day. Adults are often struck by the peaceful, orderly atmosphere that seems to flow naturally from the Montessori environment. Because the child's interaction with learning materials is relatively unmediated, the impact of a bad teacher is minimized. Discipline often consists of the teacher simply redirecting a disorderly child to a new task.

For more information on Montessori schools, see www.montes

sori.edu (the International Montessori Index) or www.montessori.org
(the Montessori Foundation), or write:

Montessori Foundation
17808 October Court
Rockville, MD 20855
800-655-5843 or 301-840-9231

Democratic/Free Schools

Democratic or free schools, growing out of the tradition begun with
A. S. Neill's experimental free school Summerhill founded in En-
gland in 1921 (still in operation) and the book he published about it
in 1961, give children almost complete freedom in their educations
and in other areas of life. Children are free to do whatever they like
in most free schools, as long as no one is hurt and property is not
damaged. Decision making is shared, with even young children entitled to a say. Free schools are as varied as the people who run them,
but generally the children decide what they would like to learn and
the curriculum is worked out between the teachers and children. In
many democratic schools (as well as in democratic classrooms in public schools), each member of the school community—kids, teachers,
administrators, and possibly parents—has one vote, and decisions,
including hiring, firing, tuition, and curriculum, are reached by voting. Some free schools encourage extensive parental participation;
others discourage parents from becoming involved.

One of the best known American free schools is the Sudbury Valley School in Massachusetts, founded in 1968. Sudbury Valley's
school principles read:

Sudbury Valley School is a place where people decide for themselves
how to spend their days.

Here, students of all ages determine what they will do, as well as when, how, and where they will do it. This freedom is at the heart of the school; it belongs to the students as their right, not to be violated.

The fundamental premises of the school are simple: that all people are curious by nature; that the most efficient, long-lasting, and profound learning takes place when started and pursued by the learner; that all people are creative if they are allowed to develop their unique talents; that age-mixing among students promotes growth in all members of the group; and that freedom is essential to the development of personal responsibility.

In practice this means that students initiate all their own activities and create their own environments. The physical plant, the staff, and the equipment are there for the students to use as the need arises.

The school provides a setting in which students are independent, are trusted, and are treated as responsible people; and a community in which students are exposed to the complexities of life in the framework of a participatory democracy.

The Sudbury Valley School
2 Winch Street
Framingham, MA 01701
508-877-3030
www.Sudval.org

The Sudbury Valley School's Web site contains a listing of other democratic/free schools. See *Free at Last: The Sudbury Valley School*, by Daniel Greenburg (Framingham, MA: Sudbury Valley Schools Press, 1987), and *The Sudbury Valley School Experience*, 3rd ed. (Framingham, MA: Sudbury Valley School Press, 1992).

For a discussion about democracy-building in public schools, go to www.egroups.com/group/DemocracyInPublicSchools.

For more information on democratic/free schools, see *Democratic*

Schools, edited by Michael W. Apple and James A. Beane (Open University Press, 1995), which contains more information on democratic public schools.

Making It Up As We Go Along: The Story of the Albany Free School, by Chris Mercogliano (Portsmouth, NH: Heinemann, 1998), is an account of an inner-city free school open to all children that has been in existence since 1969.

Finally, *Adventures on Arnold's Island,* by Arnold Greenberg, is an account of how twenty-five fifth and sixth graders created their own society and economic system backed up by fifty pounds of peanuts. You can order the book from Left Bank Press, P.O. Box 857, Blue Hill, Maine 04614, or e-mail Arnold at: mailto:grnbrg@downeast.net.

Organizations that Promote Alternative Learning

Alternative Education Resource Organization (AERO)

AERO is a nonprofit organization sponsored by the School of Living, which was founded in 1934. AERO's director, Jerry Mintz, has worked with hundreds of alternative schools and homeschool programs and is an expert on educational alternatives. AERO helps people who want to change education to a more empowering and holistic form. It helps individuals and groups of people who want to start new community schools, public and private, or change existing schools. It also provides information to people interested in homeschooling their children or finding private or public alternative schools.

AERO publishes a magazine, *Education Revolution,* that offers networking news from many different realms of alternative and holistic education. AERO also offers speaking and consulting services. See "Other 'Alternatives' Resources" for information on Jerry Mintz's book, *The Almanac of Education Choices.*

AERO
417 Roslyn Road
Roslyn Heights, NY 11577
1-800-469-4171
www.edrev.org

Creating Learning Communities

Creating Learning Communities is a book and a Web site developed by
The Coalition for Self-Learning,

> a collective of autonomous individuals and groups each working inde-
> pendently but in mutual aid to help one another promote ideas and
> actions for creating learning communities and their relevance to social
> change. Its goals and purposes are to envision a world without
> schools—a world of cooperative community life-long learning centers
> as a significant element in the emerging cooperative commonwealth
> where individuals are honoured and celebrated and where they find a
> safe place to be, to belong, to learn, and to go on developing in a mean-
> ingful way—for them, and for their whole family/community/society.

> www.creatinglearningcommunities.org

EnCompass

EnCompass offers workshops, programs, and services for educators
and families of all kinds. With an innovative focus toward stimulating
emotional and psychological health, EnCompass is nonprofit and
was founded by Ba and Josette Luvmour, authors of *Natural Learning
Rhythms.*

11011 Tyler Foote Road
Nevada City, CA 95959
800-200-1107
www.encompass-nlr.org

Paths of Learning

"We aim to inspire parents, educators, and others interested in educational policy and practice to consider diverse ways in which children and adults can gain meaningful, integrated knowledge and develop their own authentic potentials." Sponsored by the Foundation for Educational Renewal, Paths of Learning publishes *Paths of Learning* magazine, offers a free online resource center to support the growth of educational alternatives, and publishes books on holistic education.

The Foundation for Educational Renewal
Box 328
Brandon, VT 05733-0328
1-800-639-4122
www.great-ideas.org

Power to the Youth

This is an organization of youth around the nation who are taking charge of their schools, lives, and world.

"Let's face it," writes founder Bill Wetzel, age twenty:

> most schools today are some of the most boring and unhappy places around. In the words of George Bernard Shaw, "There is, on the whole, nothing on earth intended for innocent people so horrible as a school." But we don't have to spend our childhood and adolescence responding to bells, whistles, multiple-choice tests, and report cards. We can either try to improve our schools, or just not go to them in the first place! Working within the schools, we will work to increase the decision making power of students, and increase the academic freedom given to students. Imagine the ability to design your own curriculum or create your own classes! We will work on all levels to convince administrators, teachers, and parents that change needs to happen and that change is going to happen.

The Web site contains info and ideas on how students can use political action and organize to reclaim power over their own educations. www.youthpower.net

Genius Tribe

This is an organization and business started by Grace Llewellyn to support people of all ages in unschooling and other forms of self-directed learning. It offers summer camps (including Not Back to School Camp, for teenagers); a mail-order book catalog with reviews, author interviews, and book excerpts; and other events and services.

Genius Tribe
PO Box 1014
Eugene, OR 97440
541-686-2315.
www.GeniusTribe.com
www.NBTSC.org (Not Back to School Camp Web site)

Homeschooling Resources

Dobson, Linda, ed. *The Homeschooling Book of Answers: The 88 Most Important Questions Answered by Homeschooling's Most Respected Voices.* Rocklin, CA: Prima, 1998.

Griffith, Mary. *The Homeschooling Handbook: From Preschool to High School, a Parent's Guide,* revised. Rocklin, CA: Prima, 1999.

———. *The Unschooling Handbook: How to Use the Whole World as Your Child's Classroom.* Rocklin, CA: Prima, 1998.

Growing Without Schooling (GWS) magazine. Holt Associates, 2269 Massachusetts Avenue, Cambridge, MA 02140. www.holtgws.com

Jon's Homeschool Resource Page, www.midnightbeach.com/hs. (This is one of the biggest, most popular, and all around most helpful and interesting homeschooling sites on the Internet.)

Llewellyn, Grace. *The Teenage Liberation Handbook: How to quit school and get a real life and education,* revised ed. Eugene, OR: Lowry House, 1998.

www.homeschool.com lists dozens of homeschool and distance learning
   resources.

Other "Alternatives" Resources

The Parents' Guide to Alternatives in Education, by Ronald Koetzsch, Ph.D.
   (Boston: Shambhala, 1997), is a beautifully written, in-depth guide to
   options including the many different types of schools, how to choose
   a school, and even how to found your own school.
See also *The Almanac of Education Choices,* edited by Jerry Mintz (New York:
   Macmillan, 1995 and currently being updated), which includes a
   state-by-state listing of over 6,000 alternative education programs
   throughout the country. (The updated version will include over 7,500
   listings). See AERO's Web site, www.edrev.org, to order.

Index